WH... SUICIDE LEFT BEHIND

Navigating Your Own Grief Journey

Written in the first six months of suicide loss

Linzi Meaden
(co-authored by my brother in spirit)

First published in June 2021 by Paradisium Publishing

Copyright © Linzi Meaden 2021

ISBN: 978-1-9168778-0-1

This book is based on my own personal experience with suicide loss grief and is not intended as therapy.

For more information regarding this publication and other products and resources, please visit:

www.paradisium.co.uk

Contents

Dedication

Whilst this book is written with the help of my brother in spirit, it's also dedicated to him.

Stuart.......thank you for being you, for the love and kindness and encouragement you gave so effortlessly to everyone you met in your 48 years of life. You always made sure you put a smile on everyone else's face and your gift to them was a little piece of your heart, until there was nothing left to give.

Your wings were ready to take you home ....but our hearts were not.

Thank you for being the best brother I could have asked for and for being a beautiful caring son to our parents who are so very proud of you, as am I. Thank you for being a fun loving uncle to your twin niece and nephew, who you never got to see in person beyond age three and a half. They are carrying on your kind heart and selfless good deeds into future generations.

We are so very proud of you and will always love you and know that we will meet again……..we know you are enjoying paradise and thank you for all the signs you give us to let us know you are still very much around in spirit.

Acknowledgements & Thanks

To our wonderful Mum and Dad – for being the best parents and grandparents in the world.

To my husband, Chris, for his practical support and love throughout this difficult time.

To my best friend, Helen Cooper, for always being there, no matter what.

To Rob Ellen, my brother's childhood best friend, for helping to keep our childhood memories alive and for understanding grief.

To my dear friends, Millie Coates, Kelly Christmas and Katie Sermbezis, for stepping in to help me and the twins when I needed it the most. Without you, I could not have got through those tough early days.

And a heartfelt thank you to special friends who have helped or checked in on me in those early days – Mary Proctor, Peter & Julie Keen, Louise Ktoris, Kristine Moller, Destiny Krogsgaard, Claire Louise Harris, Michael Darling, Jacqueline Youldon, Tom & Bronja Whitlock, Carole & Paul Baker, Katie Haylock, Tara Sanger, Sharon Torrance, Rachel

Marwood, Michele Paradise, Kirsty Hodgson, Sue Hannibal, Darren Kidd, Kate Chapman, Charlotte Nardini, Amy Greaves, Rachel Pattison, Jane Linda, Louise Carmi, Gemma Blizard, Paul Seal, Chantal Brosens, Nina Middleton, Darren Semple, Amy Lane, Anna Chivers, Michelle Prince, Hayley Moon & Lauraine Stewart.

And finally, the special people in my brother's life, Louise (and the girls), and closest friends – best friends, Phil Ambrose, Paul Willmer & Pete Gynn, Dal Willard, Kim Willmer, Karen Bassett, Kerry & Keira Langley, William Pinnington, Debbie & Sammy, Emma J Blackman, Lauren Gynn, Pam & Susan Crowhurst, Rebecca Wheeler, Violet & Allan Crozier, Ray Parris, Rachel Emmerson, Steve Vollrath, Corinne King, Jo Davis, Vicky Stallard, John Harper. Thank you all for loving my brother. Apologies to anyone I have missed.

Katy Perkins, Phoebe Perkins and Michael Bond – we all sadly lost our loved ones during the COVID-19 lockdown locally in 2020 to suicide. This book is for you too.

It is an honour to be able to include in my book the names of loved ones

who we will all carry in our hearts forever

Remembering & Honouring Our Loved Ones Who Died By Suicide

Nicholas Baker 22	1990
Alison Sadd 50	1999
Janine Holdsworth 36	1999
Marcus Rhodes 28	1999
Dale Moden 41	2005
Jeffrey Forkings 47	2009
Alexander 16	2010
Chelsea 13	2011
Jodie "Jo" Gawler	2012
Craig Parker 43	2013

Derek Foley   2013

Jim Parker   2013

Will Beckett *42*   2013

Michael Towers *23*   2014

Yan Stuart Downie *47*   2015

Alexander "Alex" David Mullins *21*   2016

Andrew Boyle *44*   2016

Alastair Finch *35*   2017

John Chadwick *52*   2017

Teddy Fusco, Jr *41*   2017

Todd Feldman *46*   2017

Daniel Hall *18*   2018

Emily Elizabeth *24*   2018

Jack Harvey *28*   2018

Joe Damien Anderson   2018

Karl Mortimer *37*   2018

Joe Nihill 23	2020
Jonathan Smith (Jonny) 26	2020
Justin Q 20	2020
Katherine	2020
Kevin Monger 38	2020
Kieran Osborne 24	2020
Kirsty May Eales 31	2020
Leighton Dickens 39	2020
Mark Clayton 46	2020
Matthew Mackell 17	2020
Nicolas Quevedo Barrios 28	2020
Olly Beswetherick 24	2020
Paul David Perkins 58	2020
Peggy Moloney 71	2020
Richard Miles 33	2020
Sean Mark Johns 44	2020

Stuart Cooper (Stu) **48**	2020
Thomas Jesse Long **40**	2020
Janet Williams **51**	2021
Kelly Michelle Walsh **45**	2021
Tom Brown **33**	2021

I have had the privilege of connecting with the families and friends of those honoured above during my grief journey – thank you for allowing me to include your loved ones in my book – together we remember, together we are stronger.

*I apologise if there are any errors with names, ages or dates (please contact me to amend)

Foreword

"I have known Linzi for 10 years in a professional as well as a personal capacity, both of us having trained in NLP, Professional Hypnotherapy, The Havening Techniques® and more.

Her world was completely turned upside down in June 2020 when her brother died by suicide and her story needs to be shared to highlight not only the devastation of suicide, but also the trauma of sudden unexpected loss, the loss of an only sibling, the unanswered questions and the effects of the COVID-19 pandemic that currently don't include these 'other deaths' that are connected.

Having seen how she has coped with her grief since losing her brother, I truly feel that this book will help so many other bereaved families grieving loss due to suicide. Writing has helped her to process her grief and, as she has penned this book completely from the heart during the first incredibly painful six months of her grief journey, it's clear to see how she transitioned through that pain, heartache and immense loss, moving into a space of hope, acceptance, purpose and love.

Every grief journey is unique and Linzi has written this book to offer hope and a gentle guiding hand to someone like you to say you're not alone.

She is on a mission to end the stigma of suicide and for those grieving to be able to do so more openly.

Use this as a resource, for words of comfort or just to realise that someone else has been and is still going through this journey too, like you.

In my professional capacity supporting families grieving by suicide, I believe this is a must-read for anyone who has been touched by the tragedy of suicide and sibling loss."

Michele Paradise

Relationship Healer, International Speaker & Personal Development Coach for Deepak Chopra

INTRODUCTION

The global pandemic lockdown, June 2020

My brother was missing at first. One of many 'missing persons' that we hear about too often.

Just that, in itself, was an intense time of not knowing. Dealing with the police, phone calls back and forth. Waiting for news. Waiting and waiting.

Until the news finally came.

I didn't know how I was meant to grieve. I had to deal with everything as our surviving parents are both in their eighties and it was too much for them to have to cope with.

So I took it all on myself whilst also looking after three year old twins 24/7 and dealing with the COVID-19 lockdown; my husband being the sole fee-earner in the household at the time. Not only that, I had a flare-up of an autoimmune disease, most likely due to the trauma of losing my only sibling who I expected to still be in my life, living his life, for another few more decades at least.

These are the circumstances in which I was in at the time and it's so very different for each and every one of us who experiences loss through suicide.

CHAPTER 1

I'm With You

Firstly, I'm so sorry that you find yourself in this position that I'm in too.

I've written this book because writing helps me with my grief, and my one hope is that my words will somehow find a way to help you.

I started to write this three months after my only sibling died by suicide so to begin with the content is completely raw and authentic and probably highlights the rollercoaster of emotions I was going through at that time.

The book follows my personal journey through grief and describes how I dealt with all that happened over the coming months. I finished writing this at the end of 2020 – six months after he died, and I've now started on my second book which covers so much more in terms of acceptance, living alongside grief, connecting and remembering.

You can read from start to finish or just dip in and out as you need. Highlight words or paragraphs that resonate or give comfort and use the journal at the back to add memories you want to treasure forever. Just know that each word and each page is written with love and compassion for you.

I'm fully aware it takes a lot of energy to pretend to be 'OK' so give yourself permission here now to say, 'I'm not doing OK today', if that's how you really feel.

One of the many things I'm learning is that we need to stop hiding our grief for fear of being a burden to others or making others feel uncomfortable. Show your grief, share your grief. Talk about your loved one. Talk about how you feel. Let's make grief more openly acceptable and less uncomfortable. It's natural. We are human.

Everyone is going to experience grief of different magnitudes in their lives and some more than others.

With the added layer of 'suicide', it becomes all the more 'awkward' thanks to the outdated stigmas attached to that word.

I find that by speaking up about suicide, I've connected to so many others who have also lost loved ones in this way and they 'get it'. They understand the difference. They just know. Often no words are needed; the eyes say it all.

Your grief speaks volumes about how much you love your loved one. No one can ever take that away from you. Your love is what continues to connect you, even though they are not physically present. You are part of the legacy your loved one left behind. Every moment you choose to live your life with meaning, purpose, love and peace allows you to bring part of them alive again, to be beside you, in your heart, in your thoughts and in your actions. Having lost my brother, I'm also aware of how siblings tend to get forgotten, as well-wishers will more often focus on the parents, children or partners who are left behind.

So this book is dedicated to all siblings left behind…..we grieve too.

This space is for you to write the name of your loved one(s) who died by suicide. If you wish, include their relationship to you, their date of birth, the date they departed and anything else you wish to add. This is your space. You can even add a photograph. Let them be part of this book and read it with you, beside you. There's more space in the journal at the end of this book.

CHAPTER 2

Grief From Suicide – You Are Not Alone

What I've learnt is that grief is not a 'one size fits all'. No two people grieve the same. Grief can be for many reasons but, what I'm referring to here, is grief for the loss of a loved one by suicide. In my case, this is my only sibling, my older brother, Stuart, who I lost to suicide during the COVID-19 lockdown in June 2020.

I can't decide whether suicide is a choice or a decision or both, or neither of those. This is a huge topic of debate and some believe that it is purely a choice and that's OK because we believe what feels right for us. I feel that the pain they are experiencing (be it physical, emotional or other) is just too much and they believe they have exhausted all options so all that's left is to end their pain and suffering by ending their life.

They are in a state where they have to override their very own survival instincts. Their neurology is such that it's acute – a medical crisis.

A lot of circumstances align to this very point where they are mentally and probably physically exhausted. Suicide is conflicting and confusing. In that moment, the desire is peace.

I guess they think there's no other way. Perhaps they believe that by staying would cause pain to others and think that perhaps what they are about to do is best for everyone. Perhaps they don't want to let anyone down or they cannot see a way out and they just need to end it all.... They aren't selfish or cowardly. Humans are hard wired for survival and yet, they get to a point where they over-ride this natural instinct. That surely takes courage to end one's own turmoil, doesn't it?

I do also question whether suicide could be a result of possible side effects of certain medications but this is a topic for another day.

Our own personal past experiences create our present day. Every day we either reinforce our beliefs or we experience change. We are observers, both consciously and subconsciously. We hear things, we see things, we touch, taste and smell and our brains encode all of these experiences. We all live in our own unique worlds – no two worlds are the same. So, when we experience the loss of a loved one, we grieve differently too. No two people who are grieving grieve the same. A book telling us how to grieve is just based on someone's personal opinion and experiences. It may help you, it may not.

So yes, this book is based on my own personal experience alone and, as I have just said, it may resonate with you, it may not. I just invite you to read it with an open mind and take from it what you need right now and revisit it every few weeks because you may find something helpful you hadn't noticed or needed before.

When my brother died by suicide, I didn't know how to help myself or what do to.

Bereavement helplines were suggested and counsellors were offered but I didn't want to talk to strangers. I didn't want to talk to anyone like that in the early days. I just wanted to be on my own and process it all by myself. And that's OK.

'As long as I live…….you will be loved'

What I've found has helped me now after these first few months is that when I get overwhelming feelings of anxiety or emotions that I can't express in words, I use energy in motion, so I dance and sing. I couldn't do this during the first couple of months. I couldn't listen to any music and I certainly didn't want to dance. I just couldn't. But now, as I write this chapter three months in, I need to get the adrenaline from the shock out of my system. I can't let it stay inside and fester. I need to move, to change my physical and mental state that currently feels uncomfortable. Allow my heart to express itself. Energy and movement are so powerful at achieving this. I don't care how silly I may look to others.

This isn't about anyone else. This is about looking after self and allowing yourself to go with the feelings and emotions, to release whatever needs to be released at that moment in time. No part of us is ever still. We are alive. Listen to your body. Listen to your heart. Go with it. Be open.

Do what YOU need to do.

Dancing and singing reduce the stress hormone, cortisol, and creates endorphins with a steady flow of the happy hormone, serotonin. These are the feel good hormones and neurotransmitters that our mind and body need and crave at times like this.

Expressing self through music, dance, writing, talking, drawing, anything that requires movement and energy flow is so powerful. You may not feel like doing any of this right now and I get that. I didn't feel like doing anything like this at the beginning but, as time has gone on, I know the positive effect this has on my wellbeing and healing to navigate my way through my own grief journey. I hope you try this and get to experience the benefit too.

I know I'm quite fortunate because there are many others, possibly like you, who are left behind after a loved one has died by suicide in a much more difficult situation. Losing a loved one and dealing with family conflicts, illnesses, redundancy, financial problems and so much more makes grief even harder. Not that it's a competition as to who has it worse or the easiest.

Grief affects every single person individually.

No two people who are grieving grieve the same.

Grief is personal and unique and there is no timeframe to fit into or a right or wrong way to grieve. And one very important fact I learnt early on is never let anyone tell you it's time to stop grieving now and get back to 'normal' life. Anyone who suggests that clearly hasn't grieved as much as you are doing. Ask for help when you're ready or when you feel you need to. You don't need to be 'fixed'; you just need to be allowed to grieve.

This book is written to help you because I've been there and I'm still here grieving; I might just be on a different stage of my journey than you are right now.

So, whether you have just had the devastating news or you are several weeks or even months into losing a loved one by suicide, take this book as being for you from someone who has been there and wants to be by your side, guiding you through the days ahead and offering words of support, comfort and hope.

You may even be reading this because a friend has lost a loved one to suicide and you don't know how to support them and I want to personally thank you for doing this, because your support helps them more than you realise.

My hope is that I will answer some of the questions you may have and offer you support together with some tools and resources that can keep you going through each day and night.

When we lose a partner, we become widowed.

When we lose parents, we become orphaned.

There's no 'label' for anyone who loses a child or a sibling although I'm not sure labels would help anyway. Or would they?

Obviously this concept of labelling, or lack of a label, could be said for any relative but here I'm just referring to the closest of blood relatives.

As I have already mentioned, I've noticed that siblings tend to get forgotten when a loved one passes because most people will offer comfort and support to the parent, child or partner.

Losing a sibling is like losing a key part of your childhood. The one who you grew up with. That familiarity of them always just being there has gone. We are supposed to share all the special events in each other's lives and be there for each other when our parents pass away too. Grow old together but lead our own lives…..but always connected no matter what.

I have to believe that we are still connected, just in a different way now. Our bond will never die.

CHAPTER 3

My Personal Story – The Year 2020 Suicide, Grief and a Global Pandemic

At the beginning of the year 2020, life was just life. A new year. A new decade. Nothing out of the ordinary was happening. Just the usual stuff going on as a new year begins.

Sent my usual messages to my family on the 31st of December. Email to Mum and Dad wishing them a Happy New Year and a WhatsApp message to my brother saying:

'Happy New Year xxxx'

He replied an hour later:

'That's a nice photo, happy new year to you all, we have all been out for a curry and just got back x'

Everything just ordinary and familiar that gives a nice warm comforting feeling inside.

A few days later, he sent through some photos of the new car he had just bought – a BMW. My brother loves cars. I could tell he was chuffed to bits with it.

I sent him a photo of his niece in her ballet dress. *'She looks like you'* he responded.

I replied, *'They keep asking to see Uncle Stuart and Aunty Lou'* to which he answered, *'Lou is working throughout February on her days off, so it will be March x'*

I looked forward to that.

We usually messaged every one to two weeks and I sent him lots of photos and videos of his niece and nephew. He loved seeing them.

Mum and Dad were sorting out their Lasting Powers of Attorney (LPAs) at the beginning of the year and listed both my brother and me as the attorneys should we be required to make decisions for them. Once all the documents were signed, the solicitor handed over the copies and said to my Mum:

'Let's hope your kids don't go before you...'

I sent pictures to my brother of the twins playing with Meccano.

He replied saying: *'I had Meccano, do they both like it?'*

Me: *'Yes, they love it'*

My brother: *'That's useful to know for birthdays and Christmas'*

He asked whether we had been affected by the coronavirus to which I replied *'No……you all okay?'*

'Yes all fine so far, but business is very quiet, not good for my wallet……….Hopefully it will all disappear soon'

On Sunday 22 March at 4.30pm, we sent my brother a short video of his niece singing Little Bo Beep to him. *'Little Bo Beep has lost her sheep and doesn't know where to find them……'*

We sent lots of messages that week.

Early afternoon on Saturday 28 March, the twins and I did a FaceTime with him whilst he was sitting in his taxi.   We chatted for a while before one of his colleagues (and best friend) joined him in his car.   I can't remember much about that call other than thinking he seemed a little down.   The COVID situation – I could tell it was bothering him. I told my husband later that day that he seemed a bit fed up, but I didn't do anything about it because I think most people felt like that, didn't they?

On my birthday, 28 April, he sent his usual birthday message *'Happy birthday xx'* and I opened his birthday card that came in the post that contained, as was the custom, a scratch card. Didn't win anything that time but I think I won £10 on the one he had sent at Christmas.

The next day, my brother's birthday, 29 April, I sent my usual birthday messages *'Happy birthday xx'*. He replied, *'Thank you for my cards, I like the funny eyes'* because the twins had made him a birthday card with googly eyes.

This was the first year that I actually didn't send my brother a card in the post. Just a text. Not sure why. Just didn't. I regret that now.

Later that evening at 8.26 pm, I received a text saying that I had been added as his emergency contact. It was from a number I didn't recognise and I still don't know what that was connected to or why I was added.

On Monday 4 May, his niece pretended to call 'Uncle Stu' on her play telephone. I recorded her talking to him and sent a copy of the video to Stu. He replied, *'Ahh cute'*.

Fast forward to Tuesday 12 May and I saw a social media post about making clothes from the shirts of loved ones who had died. Resonated with me. Don't know why.

On Wednesday 13 May, I recorded a time lapse video of the twins putting face paints on my face. I sent it to my brother and he said, *'Wow, looks funny sped up, they should do your make up on Halloween'*. Never in a million years did I think he wouldn't be around at Halloween this year.

We continued chatting for the next couple of weeks.

On Thursday 28 May, my brother messaged to say he'd ordered an Amazon Echo Show 5 for Mum and Dad. He'd got himself one that day and decided to get one for them too, to stay in touch. Such a nice thought – an early Father's Day present perhaps (Father's Day this year being Sunday 21 June)?

Moving onto Saturday 30 May, his niece drew a picture of Nana, Grandad, Aunty Lou and Uncle Stu.......the drawing clearly shows a line going upwards from my brother's neck. Coincidence or a sign from the universe of what was to happen in exactly two weeks' time?

My brother replied, *'Very nice, did you know we have 2 rabbits now, you'll have to come down sometime x'* (obviously not allowed to at that time due to COVID).

I replied, *'Yes as soon as we are allowed, we will visit'.*

….That visit never happened.

CHAPTER 4

My Personal Story – June 2020

The Day My Brother Died,
A Part of Me Died Too

On Sunday 14 June at 7.39 am I noticed that my brother had changed his WhatsApp profile picture to something humorous.

It made me smile so I commented by saying, *'I like your profile picture ;)'*

He read it at 7.48 am but never replied. Those were the last words I sent him and the last words of mine that he read. He never replied to me ever again.

That morning, me, my hubby (Chris) and the twins went for a walk. I suggested going to Ashdown Forest but we decided to go to Bedgebury Pinetum. At about 10.50 am, my little girl became fixated by a memorial tree. She wouldn't let go and was hugging it and crying. Her twin brother kept saying he wanted to go back to the car and go home. Both were distressed which is very unusual for them. On the ground by the tree was a pair of men's sunglasses. For some reason I felt something in my heart when I spotted them, but I don't know what or why.

Back home, early afternoon around 2.30 pm I think, I thought about doing a FaceTime with my brother and the twins. For some reason, I didn't. Would life be different now if I'd made that call? We'll never know.

Later in the afternoon, I read via social media that the body of a missing local taxi driver had been found. I remember commenting how incredibly sad this was to my husband. I recall putting my hand on his shoulder as we sat outside in the late afternoon sun, thinking about the family left behind.

Before the twins went to bed that Sunday, they removed (unbeknownst to me!) some flowers from a plant and placed them in the herb garden. Orange and yellow petals, scattered among the herbs. It looked really lovely.

That evening, I watched an episode of Downton Abbey.........the one where one of the siblings dies. I remember messaging my friends saying I'd forgotten that that happened (as I'd seen it before) and saying how sad it was…..I shed a few tears.

And that was Sunday. I didn't yet know.

Unusually for me, I didn't take any photos the next day, Monday 15 June. I have 30k photos on my iPhone so that was very unusual. I can't actually remember what happened during that day either.

On Monday 15 June at 8.10 pm I received a call from my brother's partner (Lou) of two years. That in itself was highly unusual. I had a bad feeling as soon as I saw her name appear on my phone. I didn't answer.

Then I saw that she had messaged me three minutes earlier to say *'Can I ring you?'* so

I replied, *'Yes ok now'*.

I asked her what was up. I can't remember her exact words but it was along the lines of:

'Well, it's Stuart, he's missing'

My heart immediately sank. She asked if he'd done anything like this before. I said no. She then said:

'Okay now I'm really worried'

This wasn't my brother. He doesn't ever go missing. Ever.

I asked *'what happened?'* and she went into the full story of them having had a chat the previous morning (Sunday) and he then left their home in his BMW. He hadn't returned that morning (Monday) to collect his second car, a white taxi, for work. My brother never missed work. My thoughts were perhaps he was at Mum and Dad's house. She said she had just returned from driving over to our parents' house in the hope that his BMW was parked outside. It wasn't. That was what prompted her to call me. I asked lots of questions, such as what was the conversation they had about? Why? What did he take with him? How was he? We spoke for about 30 minutes. The call ended. I burst into tears. This wasn't right. Where was my brother? Was he hurt? Was he safe? Where was he?

I looked at his WhatsApp profile picture and he had changed it to the picture that Al Pacino looks at as he lies dying in the film, Carlito's Way….**'Escape To Paradise'**.

I'm sure I noticed he'd changed this sometime on Sunday afternoon and I hadn't listened to my gut at the time as to why he'd changed it. Only now had I started to realise something really bad might have happened. But I refused to think like that.

I noticed that he last looked at WhatsApp online at:

6.04 pm, Sunday 14 June 2020. Yesterday.

At 9.05 pm, Lou messaged *'I think I'll have to call the police'*. She spoke to them and they said they would call her later to chat further.

At 11.32 pm, she messaged to say the police had called back, they hadn't found any sightings of his car using cameras etc. and they were heading over to her for a chat in person.

I'm glad the twins were fast asleep in bed.

Tuesday 16 June 2020

I don't think I slept well that night. I messaged Lou at 6.15 am. She said he hadn't come up in hospital checks and in the police's opinion, his car hadn't left the local area. They had filled out a 'missing persons' report online last night.I'd sent Mum an email the previous night just asking about Father's Day presents.

I knew she would email back if my brother was there. She emailed in the morning. No mention of Stu. He wasn't there. I didn't want to worry her. I couldn't tell my parents yet that their son was missing. They are both in their eighties and very close to their first born.

At 10.00 am I received a call from the police. They wanted to go to see our parents. My husband dashed over in the car to tell them the news before the police got there but they had already arrived.

I don't think my parents had as yet taken it all in by the time Chris arrived.

At 1.30 pm I received another call from the police. They had found his BMW at the edge of Ashdown Forest. My heart sank even further.

Just after 4.00 pm, I suggested doing a 'missing persons poster' for social media. It felt so odd to even be thinking like that. Lou did the poster and added Stu's picture, the picture that would eventually be plastered everywhere online.

The police had got Sussex Search and Rescue teams carrying out an extensive search of the forest including their helicopter and drone as well as search dogs.

The police advised us not to help with the search in case of what we might find…..

I think the police were thinking the worst but I was still holding on, forever hopeful, although I was worried he was hurt or deeply sad and in need of someone to be with him. I didn't like the thought of him being alone, scared, upset, lost, lonely, afraid.

At 7.15 pm I received a call from the one of the Missing Persons Team at Sussex Police. She wanted me to agree to the release of his photo and I had to speak to Mum and Dad for their permission so I told Mum that his car had been found at Ashdown Forest. The police were now making it public, adding him to their social media accounts, reporting him as missing.

Social media went crazy. There were so many shares and comments. So many concerned people, I had no idea who they were, but they knew Stuart. They knew him and they were worried for him. Really worried. This was so out of character. I got private messages from strangers asking if they could help to search as they lived in the area. Kind, selfless people offering to help find my brother.

I was attached to my phone. Mum didn't feel comfortable about sharing his photograph publically but after several conversations, she agreed.

I hadn't eaten all day, just a few nibbles and lots of water. My mouth was dry, I was running on adrenaline.

I got only a few hours' sleep that night.

Wednesday 17 June 2020

A walker in Ashdown Forest private messaged me to say she had found a North Face baseball cap; it wasn't my brother's.

The police said it was OK for us to go to the forest today to help to look. His car had been removed from the lay-by.

Lou received a message to say someone had seen a man fitting my brother's description in Eastbourne the day before (Tuesday) so she notified the police. But that just confused things. His car was parked at

Ashdown Forest and he had apparently been seen in Eastbourne? Didn't add up.

The post by Sussex Police on Facebook had now been shared 2.5k times. I couldn't get my head around that. I also noted that two local newspapers had published his photo online too – I worried for my parents as they hadn't wanted that.

After lunch, we (me, hubby and the twins) headed over in the car to Ashdown Forest. I told the twins we were looking for a missing dog....... I had to go and do something. I couldn't wait around at home. I needed to go and look. I needed to find my brother. I needed to hold him. I needed to be there for him.

Driving down the A22, we saw loads of police cars and search teams in the lay-by where he had parked his car. It hit me, what was actually happening? People were concerned for my brother. They were looking for my brother. Why? What's going on? Where was my brother? This was serious, really serious.

We parked in the car park just further along and Lou arrived at same time. My shielding from COVID-19 had gone out of the window. I saw a couple of police officers and asked what we could do. One of them said, *'Nothing really – it's a vast area and the teams have it covered'*. It started to spit with rain. We got back in the car and drove around. I looked frantically between the trees as we drove along in the hope I might spot him or something.....a clue, a sign, something. Just something, anything.

We drove past a private road a few times and I looked towards it wondering whether we could go that way but it said private so I let it go. We parked up nearby as I thought I had spotted someone with a white top on walking amongst the trees (my brother left home wearing a white shirt).

It suddenly started to pour down heavily with rain as my hubby headed into the forest. I sat in the car with the twins. I sensed my brother was close by but I couldn't explain the feeling.

We decided to go home. The twins were restless and it was raining.

I felt glad we had at least gone. It felt like I was doing something. Seeing where his car had been parked which was now replaced by police cars triggered such strong emotions.

The police said that someone saw him sitting in his car around 3 pm on Sunday but he wasn't there when they went back.

Lou messaged me at 4.30 pm as the police had called her about a navy rucksack they had found in the forest but she told them Stu's was grey. I did think it odd that someone would just abandon their rucksack though...

That afternoon, I kept checking out the window, expecting to see a police car turn up with news. That never happened.

I was still permanently attached to my phone receiving message upon message. I had previously always been very careful to avoid using my phone in front of the twins because I wanted to make sure I gave them my full attention. This had now changed completely. I felt guilty about that. A friend messaged to say he had headed up to the forest earlier but had been told by the police that they didn't want anyone to search that day. I messaged Lou at 6.29 pm to say that this was different to what they had told us. I was confused. They were apparently calling off the search for the night. Lou didn't respond.

I checked my email and noticed Mum has just messaged at 6.38 pm to say she was really worried now and asked if I had heard anything. I didn't reply.

Two minutes later, at 6.40 pm, I was upstairs in the twins' bedroom while they were in the playroom when I got a phone call from the police. He said he was aware I had been to the forest earlier and asked if I was now at home and was anyone else with me?

I paused.......

I didn't want to hear what was coming...............I think I knew what he was about to say......but I still didn't believe this was all real.........

'Linzi, I'm sorry, I'm so sorry to tell you this over the phone............we have found a body and we believe it to be Stuart's............................he had hung himself'

The police officer sounded broken. I wanted to give him a hug.

...............those words.................my head had to try to process what I had just heard.

BAM!

My world had just collapsed.

I was shaking, he kept talking but I just ran down the stairs with the phone and out into the garden where my hubby was talking to a friend on his phone. He sensed my panic and immediately ended the call. I handed him my phone. I was crying. I was sobbing. *'I have lost my brother, I have no brother'.* I repeated this twice. *'My brother has gone. Why, why, why"*

I sat shaking, trembling, my world had just collapsed with one single phone call. I felt cold. I'd lost my brother. I didn't have a sibling anymore. Mum and Dad had lost their son, their boy. How on earth would they deal with this? The twins had lost their uncle. The only uncle they had ever known and loved so much.

My hubby continued talking to the police. They needed to go to see Mum and Dad as soon as possible. I couldn't let them do that without anyone being there with them giving them support. He offered to drive down there. I agreed. I messaged a group of my friends. I bluntly said *'My brother is dead, he hanged himself'.* I didn't know what else to say. I just needed to tell my friends. I needed their support. The twins were upstairs blissfully unaware of what was unfolding that would change their young lives too.

I pulled myself together, went indoors and helped my hubby to get things together to take to Mum and Dad's. I messaged my friends for help. I needed someone to come and be with me. I could not be by myself in the house. My hubby was going to stay overnight at Mum and Dad's. I could not be alone. My friends rallied round and, within 45 minutes, my dear friend Millie arrived on the doorstep with food supplies, gifts for the twins and a bottle of wine (or two). We hugged. I needed a hug. I relaxed a little knowing I had someone there to help me and help with the twins.

She helped to get the twins into bed and they were soon fast asleep. I was still running on adrenaline. I couldn't eat. Millie offered me a glass of wine – I couldn't drink. I just wanted water. Just water, nothing else. We sat in the living room and I briefly talked about what had happened although I was aware there was a lot of waffle and confusion coming out of my mouth. Millie just listened. She helped me to find online resources for dealing with financial affairs, funerals etc. It was all going over my head but it helped to know the information was there when I was ready for it because I didn't know what to do. What do I do? What happens when someone dies? What happens when it's suicide?

Mum and Dad wouldn't be able to deal with this. It was too much for them. I would have to do it. It was my job, my role, my responsibility. I needed to try to fix everything and make it all better.

Our lives had just been turned upside down and inside out.

Life would never be the same for any of us, ever again.

My brother had died by suicide.

CHAPTER 5

Voice Recording Transcript –Three Days After My Brother Was Found

On Saturday 20 June 2020 (three days after we were told the devastating news), my husband suggested I record myself talking about how I felt and what had happened as a way of expressing my grief.

My husband is a trauma therapist and coach, but it didn't feel right talking to him for therapy – too close to home perhaps? I don't know.

I had spent the previous couple of days talking for hours on the mobile to my brother's friends. I felt I had to keep talking for my brain to try to process and make sense of it all.

I was totally overwhelmed but also in shock. Every time I closed my eyes I had horrible visions and images and thoughts and voices filled my head up so much that I felt totally overloaded.

So, my husband's idea as a way to unravel everything that was going on in my head was to offload it onto a voice recording app. This was extremely therapeutic and I would encourage you to do the same. You may not be sure of what to say at first but, once you put aside what you think you should or shouldn't say and focus on your heart, the words will just come out naturally. Let them flow.

Whether you talk for five minutes or 50 minutes doesn't matter. This is about you being able to freely express how you feel without judgement or opinion.

I've also recorded videos online sharing my grief journey which can be found on my Facebook Page (What Suicide Left Behind) and Suicide Loss Survivors Support platform (www.paradisium.co.uk). Just like this book, I have put my pain, my heart and my soul into making these come alive. It's what keeps me going.

These are extracts from the full transcript. Totally raw and recorded 'in the moment' of being in shock, disbelief and feeling numb from what had happened.

So, this is me, explaining my experience with grief, life has changed significantly since Monday evening when

I had a phone call to say that my brother had gone missing.

...I remember the police officer said words about him. Did he say he was found hanging or he'd hung himself? I can't remember which phrase he used but I didn't think my heart could sink any lower.

I don't think I would have thought of that as a scenario .... I remember when we were out looking for my brother, searching for him when he was missing and sort of looking on the ground. I never thought of looking up at the trees for hanging so again, my heart, even though it had dropped, it dropped again further.

I sobbed, I absolutely sobbed. I couldn't believe what I was hearing. I couldn't. I think my words were "I have lost my brother. I have no brother. My brother was gone. Why why why why".

Just complete shock. And I was shaking, I was physically shaking, trembling. But my head was worrying with all these questions. What happened? I wanted to know exactly what happened. And I think I was starting to create images in my mind of where he was, what he did, how he did it, which sounds awful but that's how the mind works; I wanted to know.

....I think somebody tried to call me but I didn't take the call, or in fact no I did, I think. But I couldn't talk. So I ended the call, and then went indoors. I can't remember, in fact, what happened the rest of that evening.

....Chris went to be with my parents so I think I was on my own for about 15 minutes, but I just tidied up the house. I had to keep busy, I had to keep my mind busy, I couldn't sit, and also for the twins, I had to be very mindful of them seeing me because I didn't want them to know right away what had just happened. My friend turned up, I think we hugged, a big squeezy hug. We're not allowed to hug anybody for months apart from anyone in our household. And I just thought sod COVID – I was still in shock. My shielding sort of went out the window.

..... I was basically scrolling through [online] and telling everyone who was out looking for him and searching and helping. I was going through and telling them "sorry it's bad news". And that took a lot of work to go through; that took a long time to do that.

.....Was he really so depressed? Was life really that bad? What had just happened, it was surreal. Every time I shut my eyes, the images of the forest of where

his car was parked, I was running through different scenarios of what he did. Where did he go? How did he do it? It's awful to think that but that's what was going on in my head. Every now and again I'd start trembling, shaking and be cold, shivering. My head was just full, absolutely full of questions. And obviously people bombarded me with questions too.

...And it was incredibly difficult, I think I went to bed at 11 o'clock. And I did not close my eyes until must have been gone 4 am that morning. And then I opened them again, about 7 am, so three hours sleep, which I think is pretty good, under the circumstances. That morning, my eyes opened, I mean I had barely slept so it wasn't a case of I'd forgotten it had happened and was the dream, it was very much I knew exactly what had happened, it was very real then.

And I think that the key was keeping myself busy. Feelings of just complete disbelief of shock, of needing answers. And I just did not want to be by myself when my husband stayed overnight with my parents. So we arranged for when Millie who stayed overnight had to go home, for another friend to come over and she brought her eight month old baby, which is what I needed. I held her. Just cuddling babies is so therapeutic, just for that brief, brief moment it was just calm. Quiet. Authentic. It was sort of a human connection with a small human that had nothing other than just pure love, authenticity. No words, just the way she looked at me. She touched my face, she kept giving me kisses on my face, she clearly totally understood I was very hurt and sad, and she knew that. It was amazing, it helped so much so that I can't remember the rest of the day.

So, this would have been Friday, this would have been yesterday but it feels busy, as each day goes on these things are now more distant. So even though I'm talking about yesterday. I can't actually really remember much about it. It feels like it was a week ago. But it was only yesterday. Bit of a blur. My eyes are searching for clues as to what happened. And, again, struggling to eat, running on adrenaline. I'm somebody who has to eat regularly. I can't not have breakfast, lunch, dinner, snacks, I have to eat and yet I haven't been able to eat.

.....Oh, my husband went to collect my brother's things on Thursday afternoon from the house and then Friday afternoon brought back his rucksack which he had with him in the forest, and his phone and wallet and all that. And these are just the certain things I wanted to hold and touch and just think, wow, they

were the last things with him. It is a strange feeling, very strange.

...Drinking loads and loads of water as keep getting a dry mouth. Even though I'm drinking lots of water and my head hurts. I never get headaches and my head has been absolutely hurting. In fact, from the moment of him going missing. My head was hurting with all the wanting to know why, what's going on, what's happened, where is he? And then there's obviously the news of being told he's gone. Head absolutely hurting. Absolutely hurting.

....I felt that even though I wanted people around me because I didn't want to be on my own, I did want to just take myself off to a room and be by myself and I can't, I couldn't really do that with the twins. But I still desperately feel that I want to. In fact, I'm sitting in a room now all by myself whilst Chris is feeding the twins downstairs so I can do this but it's actually quiet, I like the quiet. I don't want any TV, we've had no TV on, no films, we normally watch a movie or a series in the evening and I just do not want to look at the TV, I don't want to hear noise. I don't want noise, I want quiet. I think because my head is just overloaded. So we put on some nice relaxing piano music which is nice but I prefer quiet right now.

...And every night I've cuddled a teddy bear in bed which has been so comforting to cuddle and hug, something that's really helped. And I'm sure that's what's given me, even though it's 3 or 4 hours, sleep. I don't think I would have got that, if I hadn't been hugging my teddy bear. But I've surprised myself how I've kept going. I haven't collapsed, I surprised myself. I don't know. I'm running on autopilot, on adrenaline. I have to keep myself busy, sorting out the funeral arrangements, the funeral directors and I've sorted stuff, I've done emails, I've kept myself busy, busy, busy because I felt at the moment that's what I need to do, but I know also I do want to just do nothing.

....But we've got to get so much done and there's not really anybody else that can do it. And it's not fair for our parents to have to go through this and do things and Chris has been doing so much stuff as well and trying to run a business, trying to look after us, trying to help with fetching things, going to my parents, getting things from the police station and from Stu's house. So he's exhausted, absolutely exhausted.

...It's such a heavy cloud, grief, of everything, absolutely everything and I'm actually amazed I'm sitting here talking, I'm not crying. I've been through so many photographs, messages from people.   Every

time I'd pick up the phone and look at messages or photos, I would cry. But now, as each half day comes by, I feel that I'm further away from those images that I was running through the movie in my mind.

Messages now when I read them; they're not as raw as they were those first few days, everything was so raw, so incredibly raw.

And so emotional, and as each half day goes past, I feel that I'm able to deal with it, my head seems to be getting in a better place to deal with it all.

So, we're now Saturday afternoon, almost Saturday evening.

I feel that I could probably eat something for dinner tonight, and maybe even have a glass of wine. Normally every night in this pandemic I've been having a glass of wine but I've absolutely not wanted any alcohol whatsoever, only water and tea.

I remember Chris asking if I wanted a cup of tea. When I first heard about Stu, I think I asked for tea with sugar in it just, just to take the edge off.

I don't normally have sugar in tea, but this is what they do in the movies, don't they.

...The next challenge is tomorrow we're going to tell the twins they've lost their uncle. We need to deal with that.

They know something's happened. And they've seen me upset and they know something and we've got to explain tomorrow.

...So, yeah, this is just a weird, strange situation. I feel that I've turned a corner, I feel the worst days, I'm hoping the worst days are behind me now.

So, we found out he died on Wednesday and it's Saturday afternoon now. That might sound quite fast. For some people it might sound, like, "Nope, you're going to be experiencing a whole new range of emotions over the next coming days and weeks and months ahead".

I don't know, I don't know what to expect. This is all new to me.

I can visually see in my mind the images I was creating of my brother of going through the woods. Before, that image was right up there, right close in front of my eyes; it was a big image. When I keep trying to bring that back it's much further ahead in front of me and it's more distant and I think that's why

I'm not as emotional because the emotions. I'm detaching from emotions. I've been doing Self Havening (a trauma release technique).

...And the night actually when I was told he had died. When I heard, I was too weak to actually move my hands, or my arms, and I visualised myself Havening without using my arms. And I think that is what actually got me off to sleep, just after four o'clock that that morning. I was visualising being Havened myself. And that helped to release the oxytocin, the serotonin, which is what I needed.

The Havening has helped massively and I will continue to do that as often as I need just purely just stroking my arms and nothing more than that, nothing more than that. I've been humming tunes just every now and again just to sort of brighten myself up or to clear my head.

If my head's busy with thoughts, just humming a tune makes such a big difference.

...And I've had to carry around a notebook because of the many calls from different people. The coroner's office, the funeral director, the police, friends and my parents.

...We've got my brother's phone that we can't get into at the moment because of the passcode so that's something, right now, that's absolutely crucial, if we can get into the phone, so that's a real hope. I don't know what, if we do get in, what we're going to find, whether it's going to help or not, I don't know. But if we can do that.

...I've been absolutely blessed and overjoyed by people's kind words, generosity, there's so many posts from people and friends of his and everyone saying what an absolute gentleman he was, the bestest of friends, he was caring, he was kind. He was always there for others, and yet....we couldn't be there for him, he was a very private person.

And he was brilliant with people, absolutely brilliant with people, they loved him. They absolutely loved him and I feel very proud that that's my brother, so, so proud.

...I'm amazed I've spoken for this long before getting really upset. It's like looking at pictures. Initially, they were so emotional to look at but now looking at photographs it provides comfort. It's comforting. When I started hearing everyone's comments again it

was very emotional to read it and now I'm reading it and it's providing comfort.

...Doing this recording, having a shower every morning, is helping, just to stand under the shower and just wash it all away and I've made sure I've got myself dressed every day and I've not put much make-up on, but enough just to not scare myself looking in the mirror.

...I can't go out anywhere at the moment. I just want to stay, stay here, stay home. I know I've got lots of things I want to sort through, photographs and possible things of his that I've got that we've had from childhood, I think I might have some things.

But I feel now, I feel that I can start thinking about how we can celebrate his life. Can we do a bench for him along the seafront or somewhere where people can go and sit and be with him? And his best mate wants to plant a tree. My little girl was hugging a tree that Sunday morning when he left home, distressed, and she would not let go. And she's got such a bond with her Uncle Stu. I believe that she felt pain. She felt distress, sadness, heartbreak and she was hugging that tree. And I really believe that, so I want to plant a tree in his memory and we're going to have a bench arranged and I'm also going to get some teddy bears arranged made out of his shirts. So, all these things are actually quite nice to look forward to. I feel that all this, we can do some good now, we can do some good things, in the local community he was clearly loved and clearly loved as a son, as a brother, as a friend.

...And I feel now I can understand about death more when other people go through it, I can relate, whereas before I've felt I've never been able to really relate but now I've been there, I have seriously been there; I'm here now.

...I remember, repeating myself, saying "I have no brother, my brother's gone, there's nobody now". When our parents pass, our little family unit, the four of us, it's just me, I've got no one to share those memories of growing up as kids, you know, to think that he's not going to be around.

...But then equally, what I've thought, which I think has helped is that, do you know what, this world at the moment is kind of in a pretty bad place and actually he's probably in a better place. He's in paradise. He's in a good place. He hasn't got to grow old and suffer. Whatever the world is going to bring us, illnesses and

struggles; that's ended in his life, he's gone to a good place. He's happy, he's happy, whilst we are, you know, coming to terms with everything, the adjustment and everything. I feel that he's safe, I feel he's safe now, nothing can harm him anymore. I haven't got to worry about him now. And I feel that I did perhaps think there was sadness behind his eyes, even though he was always laughing and smiling, it's often the case because people put on a front but there was sadness behind his eyes. I think I feel comforted in the knowledge that he can't come to any harm now and I know that when I go, he's there, he's there waiting. And so, when I think of it like that, it really helps, it really really helps. And he's always now with me. He's my guardian angel and a guardian angel for the twins.

...I have yet to see the white feather. Whenever there's been things significant in my life, white feathers have appeared.   So, Stuart, please can you present somewhere a white feather or perhaps you're doing something else which is a little bit more your style, I don't know what, but I look forward to seeing whatever it is just, it's just a way of you saying hello, really really would love that a lot..."

CHAPTER 6

The Funeral – July 2020

Within a week of my brother passing, I needed to arrange his funeral. It was too much for our parents to do so I took on this task.

I had never arranged a funeral before. I had no idea what to do.

I asked friends for recommendations and searched online. There were many funeral directors to choose from so I went with my gut feeling and I actually found a company that was in the building next door to the taxi office where my brother worked so I took some sort of comfort in this. Perhaps they knew my brother? I don't know. But I rang them and the lady who answered was extremely professional and understanding, talking me through the whole process and even giving me space when I burst into tears.

As this was during the COVID-19 restrictions we were unsure about whether funerals were going ahead and how many mourners we could invite. I think it started off that we could only invite 10 people then this increased to 20. Mum's birthday was close and she didn't want the cremation of her son to be too near that date, so we opted for Friday 10 July which was a few days before her birthday.

We wanted to make sure my brother's funeral was how he would have wanted it to be. He didn't leave a will or an expression of wishes so it was left to us to make the decisions. Being the fun person he was, we needed to add humour and colour.

The choice of music was based totally on his own taste. He loved driving. He loved cars. He used to love Madness when he was a kid. So the first piece of music, 'I Like Driving in My Car' by Madness, seemed appropriate and fun!

The next piece, something to reflect on during the service, needed to be more gentle and soothing. Apparently, he loved 'Summer Breeze' by the Isley Brothers so we went with this. And finally, we had to choose something from his beloved Guns N' Roses.....and what could be more fitting that 'Paradise City' seeing as this is the image he left behind on his phone when he departed, 'Escape to

Paradise'. Little did we know that at the funeral, the music was played quite loudly and this was a bit too much for our parents at the end. But, it was for Stuart and I'm sure he was laughing at us all listening to this heavy metal, especially as Mum and I are more used to Il Divo!

The next task to undertake was the Order of Service but the funeral directors arranged this as part of the service they offered. I felt it wasn't enough to have just this one memorial booklet, I wanted to do a 'Celebration of Life' booklet to give to everyone who attended.

So I got straight to work and found a software programme with a template to create a montage of photographs and words and poems.

It was an extremely cathartic thing to do and kept my mind busy. Through tears, both happy and sad, I created something that I felt Stuart would be chuffed with. It was then printed and I was pleased with the result.

My best friend organised for seedlings to be put in handmade envelopes that she had created which bore an image of my brother and the poem 'A Limb Has

Fallen From the Family Tree' to be sent to me. We wanted everyone to plant a small tree in their gardens in his memory.

An announcement was placed in the local press in print and online to let people know the details of his funeral.

His best friends and colleagues wanted to arrange a cortege of their taxis on my brother's final journey. One of my brother's favourite places was at Galley Hill in Bexhill-on-Sea so we decided that the hearse would make its way to the top of the hill and the taxis would all follow on the funeral route towards the crematorium.

We put ribbon around the wing mirrors on our cars to show our respect to the beautiful life that had been lost. Yellow ribbon represents suicide prevention awareness and gold was the colour of his beloved BMW so we opted for a golden yellow ribbon. It was our way of saying we were all together for my brother, supporting him on his final journey to paradise. Saying thank you for being such an important part of our lives. Honouring him and everything he did with such kindness and compassion.

On the days leading up to his funeral, I simply had no idea how I was going to get through it, let alone everyone else. Having seen how devastated so many of his friends were, I knew this would be so incredibly difficult for them too. And for our parents, they shouldn't have to be attending their son's funeral. I tried to put it all out of my mind and focus on each day rather than the date of the funeral.

But three weeks went by and suddenly it was Friday 10 July. The sun was shining.

We had chosen not to have the twins with us and fortunately a kind friend came to the house to look after them. All they knew was that we were going to say goodbye to their uncle.

We set off in our car for the one hour journey which took us through so many places where we had spent our late teenage years and into adulthood.

Driving a route that I would normally take when heading to Mum and Dad's suddenly had a very different meaning. This route was like a slideshow of past memories. So many reminders popped into my head as we drove along, things I hadn't thought of for years. It was so painful to be thinking 'I'm driving to my brother's funeral'. This wasn't real, surely. Why was this happening? My brother had driven up and down these roads for decades. And now he's not here. Why? Why is he not here anymore? It was tough. And we hadn't even got to the funeral director's yet.

Up until this day, I hadn't actually been to see my brother in the Chapel of Rest. I really wanted to initially but then the funeral director said I wouldn't be able to see his face because, since he had been outdoors in all weather for three days and three nights, he was in a closed coffin. I later asked if I could hold his hand but she said it would probably be best if I didn't as he had now been deceased for a few weeks. So, on the morning of his funeral, I knew that this was my only chance to say goodbye to him.

My husband dropped me off outside the funeral directors and I went in, not really knowing what to expect. I was welcomed by the funeral director who led me to the Chapel of Rest. As the door opened and I walked inside and turned my head, I saw his coffin by the window. I froze and burst into tears. Oh my goodness. My brother was in that box. I asked her to stay with me for a bit. I didn't quite know what to do other than to go over to him and put my hand on his coffin. I remember wanting to hug him and talk to him and hear his voice and to hold his hand. But I couldn't, could I. So I put both my hands on the coffin and shook it………..I wanted to check he was in there. I was surprised at how heavy it was. I tried to imagine where his face was. I told him I loved him.

I'm in absolute tears writing this…….

But I'll keep going.

I just stood there with him. I was aware that I had limited time. I wish now that I'd been to see him earlier but at least I was there now.

My husband came into the room. I knew it was time for my brother's final road trip, his journey home.

I put two silly childhood toys on top of his coffin. I knew it would make Stu laugh. One was 'Flat Eric' the yellow thing from the Levi adverts, and the other was orange Tango man – an orange rubber man thing that he'd kept all these years from the late 1990s.

I also added the road sign I had made up that said:

'Paradise Way – Route 66. Stu Cooper RIP'

They were just silly items but I knew in my heart that this was exactly what he would have wanted.

I looked at the plaque on his coffin. Just seeing his name. And the date. It was the date he was found, not the date we believe he died, but it was too late to change this now.

I said goodbye and gave him one last 'hug'.

Outside, I stood by the hearse waiting for the flowers to be placed inside and eventually the coffin. It felt so surreal.

Standing there, watching those people carrying my brother into the back of a hearse. I suddenly felt very protective of him. I needed to be with him on his final journey. I was the grown up now. I had to step up to this task.

Mum and Dad were heading straight to the crematorium as it would be too emotional for them to join the cortege.

The hearse was ready. We got in our car and waited for it to drive past so we could follow on behind. I still could not believe what was happening.

We followed around the little streets and towards the seafront. I started to notice people standing at the side of the pavements, watching and bowing their heads.

Some were crying.

I had no idea who these people were but they must have known my brother.

As we approached the bottom of Galley Hill, that's when I just couldn't control my tears. All his taxi driver friends were parked up on either side of the road standing, waiting. They all looked so incredibly upset and shocked still. They had lost their colleague, their friend, their best buddy.

I then saw Stuart's partner and her family – all in tears – also in disbelief at what they were witnessing.

As we drove slowly to the top of the hill that overlooked the Sussex coast, we paused, then turned our vehicles around into the direction we had just come and descended back down again, my brother's friends bowed their heads in respect and then got into their cabs to follow behind on Stu's final journey. There were about 30 cars altogether.

Stu, I hope you saw this and realised just how much you were loved and respected.

I had the window down and I thanked people who were patiently quietly waiting at the sides of the roads we passed.   I wanted to reach out and just hug everyone.

The journey was beautiful.   Stu's favourite places along the coast and I think it took about 45 minutes as we headed towards the crematorium at Eastbourne. By coincidence, he actually lived almost opposite this so, as we approached the crematorium, more people stood at the roadside paying their respects too.

He should be driving home, turning right here, not turning left into the crematorium in a box.

I knew our parents were waiting. The hearse made its way slowly to the entrance of the Chapel of Rest and I literally jumped out of our car before my husband could park up as I needed to walk behind the last few metres of the hearse's journey. I saw Mum and Dad and went straight over to them to give them a hug. It was heartbreaking, so incredibly heartbreaking.

Nobody else was hugging due to the COVID-19 restrictions that were in place but I couldn't not hug our parents on a day like today, could I?

The music started up 'I Like Driving in My Car' and the pall bearers lifted the coffin up and carried my brother into the Chapel.

The service was being streamed live online to those who were unable to be there due to the restrictions limiting the number of attendees at a funeral.

I sat with my husband, next to Mum and Dad. Stuart's friends made their way to seats and we all sat and waited.

In front of us all was Stuart's body, resting in his coffin. Mum and Dad's wreath placed perfectly on top.

Son, brother, uncle, best friend, partner, colleague…he was something to everyone there. We sat there still not really believing he had taken his own life. Expecting him to walk through the doors and say, 'fooled you'. If only….

The celebrant began to speak. We had opted for a non-religious service as that's what Stuart would have wanted. It was very moving. There were some funny moments…..and some sad moments.

It all seemed to be over very quickly and the curtain began to draw around his coffin. Guns N' Roses started playing (too loudly!) and we needed to leave the Chapel and get into the fresh air. We eventually made our way to the memorial gardens where all the wreaths and tributes were beautifully laid out for us to see. And that was it. That was my brother's funeral.

How did we just get through that? I've no idea, but we did. We all did. I hope Stu is proud of us all.

Ashes

My brother loved nature. He loved the outdoors, hiking, walks, animals, plants etc., so to have his ashes kept indoors didn't feel right but neither did scattering them in just one place because he was a free spirit and he needed to be free in the places that were meaningful to him and to us. So we have scattered his ashes in seven different places and we feel this was the most fitting and appropriate way not just for us as a family but also for Stuart.

In addition, both Mum and I have had jewellery made that contains some of his ashes as this feels like a part of him is physically with us every day.

CHAPTER 7

A Fallen Limb…

A friend sent me this poem and we used it for my brother's funeral. It's definitely one of my favourites and has a special meaning.

A limb has fallen from the family tree.
I keep hearing a voice that says,

'Grieve not for me.
Remember the best times,
the laughter, the song.
The good life I lived, while I was strong.

Continue my heritage,
I'm counting on you.
Keep smiling and surely the sun will shine through.

My mind is at ease,
my soul is at rest.
Remembering all, how I truly was blessed.

Continue traditions,
no matter how small.
Go on with your life, don't worry about falls.

I miss you all dearly,
so keep up your chin.
Until the day comes, we're together again.'

– Author Unknown

CHAPTER 8

How Grief Feels After Four Months

I'm sitting here at my desk, Stu's photo looking at me, it's raining outside.

I'm crying. I don't know why. I was feeling upbeat and positive and happy this morning. I felt energised, alive and purposeful.

But then I suddenly had an overwhelming feeling in my heart. I can't explain it. I suddenly felt the need to escape from everything. I felt lost, alone, afraid, sad, heartbroken......

I needed a hug. Not just a quick hello hug. A proper hold, embrace, connection, feeling the other person's heartbeat hug. Feeling love and strength and support. Feeling safe. Feeling held. Just to take me away from everything right now. It's all OK. Everything is going to be OK. Human connection. The need to breathe again. To find that inner strength again. To rebuild the happy. To feel OK. Again. To release and just let go. To hold space. No words, no nothing. Just a hug. For as long as it's needed to make all the difference. Minutes or hours. Doesn't matter. Hugs. Hugs are what we all need right now.

Nearly four months since Stuart ended his life and I feel like I'm running out of memories or things that almost feel like they bring him back. Over the last few months I've been finding photographs I'd forgotten about, learning about his life from his friends, connecting with those who loved him. And now that feels like it's coming to an end. …….. But this is what has helped me. All of these moments, conversations, memories, discoveries; they have kept me going.

What do I do when it stops? What do I do?

- I want to plant a tree

- Write a poem

- Write a piece of music

- I want to keep talking about him and hearing about him and learning new things that I didn't know

- I want to be OK

- I want to help our parents

- I want to carry on my brother's incredible kindness

- I want to make him proud that I'm keeping going and holding our little family unit together and looking after Mum and Dad, as he did

- I want to smile again

- I want to know his friends are doing OK

- I want to be braver

- I want to feel safe

- I want to love more

- I want to help those who need help

- I want to finish what he started (he'll guide me as to what this is)

- I want to feel loved unconditionally

- I want to make the most of every moment

- I want to donate to charities in his memory

- I want to run

- I want to turn my pain into a purpose

- I cannot waste my life; I'm living for me and for my brother

CHAPTER 9

The Inquest – November 2020

The purpose of an inquest is to establish four key things: the identity of the deceased as well as where, when and how they died.

From my earlier conversations with the Coroner's Officer, I knew there would be an inquest at a later date, probably around six months after my brother's death.

With the first lockdown having been followed by the second one in October, I began to worry that it might be moved until after Christmas.

But the call came to say we could go ahead and book the inquest for a date in a few weeks' time, this being 10 November. Coincidentally, while Stu's funeral was days before Mum's birthday, his inquest was just days before Dad's birthday.

I was made aware that there was a strong possibility the local press would be in attendance, which they currently have every right to do.

This immediately made me feel distressed, being aware of what some journalists had written up after other inquests held for death by suicide. I'd seen it impact upon their loved ones left behind and I think it's so wrong that they are continued to be allowed to do this. It's just unnecessary additional pain inflicted upon the families and all because the press believe the public have a right to hear everything about the person who ended their life. It's wrong, just wrong. This should be the family's choice and decision, not anyone else's.

I was informed that I could request advanced disclosure which meant I would receive all the paperwork, bar the photographs, in advance of the hearing.

I said yes to this as I wanted to be prepared and not be shocked by anything on the actual day.

So, a few days before the date, an email arrived to which the documents were attached. I didn't want to open it up.

I waited a few hours and then I clicked on each attachment not really knowing what I was about to read.

Toxicology Report

Pathology Report

Post Mortem Report

Witness Statement

GP Medical Report

Police Statements

I read each one. I was already aware of the toxicology and pathology reports having already spoken to the Coroner's Office about these.

I think the report that shook me the most was the one that contained the police statements as these were quite detailed in terms of how he was found and what happened in those moments.

I knew I had questions so I wrote them down and sent an email to the Coroner's Office. Initially it was just going to be a police officer who would be called to the stand at the hearing but, after reading my questions, it was decided to call the GP as well.

On the day of inquest, my husband had to stay with the twins so I went along with my brother's childhood best friend, Rob, who now feels like a long-lost brother in some way but obviously he is no relation.

We were only allowed four people at the hearing due to the lockdown restrictions so it was myself and Rob plus Lou with her Mum for support.

When we arrived at the location, it was cold, wet and windy.

We headed into the building and were directed to the room where we were fortunately allowed to remove our face masks as we were sitting two metres apart from each other, compulsory at that time due to COVID-19.

I was relieved, so relieved to find that there was no press there. The relief on my face must have been readily noticeable because I had feared what they would publish.

I handed out thank you cards that I'd made for the police officers, the Search & Rescue Team and the Coroner's Office. I just felt I wanted to say thank you in some way for helping to find Stuart.

The Coroner appeared, a retired solicitor I believe, and we all sat down. It was very official and formal.

He began with his condolences and then continued with the hearing. He read out parts of the statements and reports. He asked if we had any questions so I had the opportunity to ask mine. I wasn't overly keen on his responses though.

As a family, we wanted the date of his death to be changed to 14 June, instead of the 17 June when he was found. The Coroner said no because the actual date wasn't known even though we were 99.9% certain he did take his own life on 14 June. This upset me.

The police officer read his statement from the stand. The GP then read his statement and we asked a few questions but he really couldn't answer these which was understandable.

And then the Coroner concluded that Stuart took his own life by suspension.

Case closed.

And that was that.

Those 'official' people who had suddenly appeared in my life almost from the moment of Stuart having gone missing and being found had closed the file and moved on to other things. They had other deaths and cases to deal to focus on; that's their job. Coroner's Officer, police, funeral director......marked as completed.

So what do we do now?

What's next?

I'm aware that Stuart's inquest was relatively 'straight forward'. Some inquests can take a year or more before they are heard due the complexities of the death and can continue for days or weeks, and of course this just adds to the 'additional layers' of grief and stress that suicide loss brings. If you have been through this or are going through this, my heart goes out to you.

It's been five months since you died Stuart. I think the reality is starting to kick in. Whilst the initial shock and trauma have lessened, the realisation of what has actually happened and all the events, emotions, feelings, hazy days, busy days, sleepless nights have all grouped together and it feels like they have been dumped by my feet. I stand and look at this sack of the past five months and wonder............do I pick it up and carry it around with me? Do I step over it and walk away? Do I open it up and go through it all? Or is there another option?

I've chosen the 'other option' because it's the unknown and I'm not sure what the future holds.

So I'm taking it one day at a time, sometimes, one moment at a time. One thought at a time. Always remembering to slow down and breathe.

I feel like I cannot and will not let his death go without something purposeful and beneficial coming out of it. His life on this earth has ended but mine still exists and I don't know how long that will be for. So, for as long as I continue living, I will continue loving my brother and keeping his memories alive and bringing his kindness back to life.

I'm stubborn. Like Stuart. I won't be told what to do from now on. If I want to share how I feel, I will. I'm not holding back my grief to avoid making others feel uncomfortable.

Grief isn't something to be ashamed of and neither is suicide. If you prefer to grieve in quiet, then that's what you need to do. If you prefer to talk and share about your grief, then that's what you need to do. If it's a mixture of both, then that's what you need to do.

I had no idea how grief impacts on a person, until now. My grief journey is unique to me, just as your grief journey is unique to you. And we will all have more than one grief journey, often overlapping. But, one thing is for certain, grief does not end. It's part of you and, whilst it may become more compact in years to come, don't ever let anyone tell you to get over it. Grief is lost love...love with nowhere to go. It's the what was, the what could be, the what ifs and the what's next. It transforms with you as you transform.

CHAPTER 10

What is......Suicide & Grief?

Although I'm trained as a mind coach, I'm new to suicide and grief on a personal level. This is just my research and understanding of both.

What is suicide?

Suicide is 'ending your own life'. People who are in inescapable pain or unbearable suffering may want to end their life to end that pain and suffering. When someone ends their own life, we say that they 'died by suicide'.

In the UK, we no longer say 'committed suicide'; this hasn't been used since 1961. It's discouraged by mental health professionals and specialists in suicide prevention. 'Commit' is associated with crime (in the justice system) and sin (in religion). This term can deepen the emotional pain surrounding a suicide death. I prefer 'died by suicide' or 'ended their life'.

In addition, words such as successful, unsuccessful, completed and failed should be avoided when describing a suicide or suicide attempt, together with similar language that either romanticises or stigmatises the act.

Using language that criminalises the act is highly insensitive to those whose lives have been affected by suicide. I have heard the phrase, 'committed suicide' and similar a lot. Some from innocence or ignorance and some from those who believe it is a crime.

Suicide is still a hard subject to broach. I'm on a mission to change that.

Let's make it OK to talk about suicide; studies show that discussing suicide with someone will not make that person suicidal or increase the likelihood of acting on suicidal ideation. However, I've also read studies that suicide increases after the death of a celebrity by suicide....

The World Health Organization (WHO) estimates that around 800,000 people die from suicide each year. These 'people' are our brothers, sisters, sons, daughters, mums, dads, husbands, wives, partners, aunts, uncles, friends, colleagues..... Never did I think my brother would be one of the statistics and often wonder whether he would ever have thought this too….?

One person dies from suicide every 40 seconds. Some sources predict this will increase to one death from suicide every 20 seconds since the pandemic.

And, along with those who die by suicide, there are many more who attempt suicide and survive.

Some then carry on with life but tragically some will make many more attempts. Shockingly, the third leading cause of death for teenagers between 15 and 19 years is suicide.

And, whilst you are reading this book, more families, just like mine and yours, will be experiencing the acute pain of losing their loved one to suicide.

This is happening now.

The effects on families and friends from a death by suicide are long-lasting and life changing.

WHO recognise suicide as a public health priority. It's tragically too late for our loved ones who have died this way.

However, I'm now making it my purpose to make a difference to, even if just one life is saved as a result.

What is grief?

'Intense sorrow, deep distress, especially caused by someone's death'

I didn't know what to expect with grief and I found many different 'models' as to what the stages of grief are.

I personally didn't experience and don't experience grief as in this linear description (although it should be highlighted that the following was actually intended as stages for dying by cancer and not actually grief, but it's been adapted over the years by the field of psychology to try and fit it in with grief):

Denial

Anger

Bargaining ('if only' statements)

Depression

Acceptance

Plus the newest 'stage', Finding meaning/purpose

And for grief from suicide loss, there's the additional emotions of:

Shock

Anger

Guilt

Despair

Confusion

Feelings of rejection

And many more.

Suicide grief is complex. Time itself doesn't heal. That's my viewpoint at this particular moment but I know everyone has a different opinion. I may have different views in a year's time and that's OK because I'm learning as I go along. Beliefs change. And that's OK.

I'm finding my own way and making my own relationship with both suicide and grief. I was never expecting them to be in my life, but they are here now, and they are not going anywhere. So I might as well work together with them, instead of against them, because that will only cause me more pain and suffering if I don't.

How many of these have you experienced or are experiencing?

Flashbacks

Nightmares

Panic attacks/anxiety

Social withdrawal

Feeling alone

Scared

Not understood or heard

Creating in your mind what happened

Searching for answers, clues.

The stigma of suicide (it's a selfish act etc.)

These are all quite common as a result of loss by suicide. In another chapter, I list various suggestions as to how you can help yourself and, of course, speak to your GP or therapist if you feel unable to do this by yourself. You are important and you must take care of you.

What I hear so often is that those who die by suicide were the kindest souls on this earth. They often went out of their way to help others and yet, in their time of need, who was there for them? This can cause those left behind to feel immense guilt.

I personally feel that my brother felt he didn't have a choice at that moment in time for reasons we will never know and that it was an impulsive decision. A permanent decision to a possibly temporary situation perhaps?

CHAPTER 11

The Ocean of Grief

When I think about my own grief, I look at it like this....

At first, a huge wave hits you from behind, almost knocking you off your feet and flooding you with every emotion possible.

Then another wave hits but this time it's a bit smaller and you kind of expected it.

You need to find a boat to settle in to see clearly all around you and feel safe.

You find your boat and set sail. Ripples still remain from those big waves in the ocean. Every now and again a slightly larger wave rocks the boat, but you hold on. You hold and keep paddling.

You see a storm cloud ahead and you know the only way forward is to go through it. You have to be brave to get to the other side. So you brace yourself, you paddle like crazy, exhausting yourself but somehow you keep going. The storm is fully upon you and you are physically and mentally drained. You want to give up. But you don't. You know you are almost through the other side. You can actually see calmer waters in the distance. You allow yourself to go with the ocean waves. You settle into your boat and let the waves carry you. The storm cloud passes and is behind you now. A rainbow appears. There's a ray of sunshine, giving you hope.

Your boat is still, in the calm waters. You breathe. You reflect on everything you've just been through and wonder how on earth you managed it, but you did. You did.

Out of nowhere, a wave appears and rocks the boat so much that you fall out. You're in the water. Where did that come from? Totally unexpected. But you have to get back into your boat.

You have to find a way. Instead of blaming the ocean or the boat for tipping you out, you focus on helping yourself to get back into the boat. Once you've thrashed about in the water, letting out all your anger and upset and tears, you breathe. You feel a wave coming up behind you and as it does, it gently raises you up so you just reach out and you're back in your boat. You actually turn around and thank the wave for helping you.

You set sail in all weathers. And the waves match your emotions. You are one. You are the universe.

Some days, the water is clear and blue and you can see life beneath the ocean. It's beautiful, calm, tranquil and comforting.

Other days, there are ripples of waves that come and go.

And on other days, a wave might appear, sometimes you expect it and other times it's totally out of the blue. But you know you've been through the worst days now and you can keep going.

You and your boat. It's your boat and no one else has been on that journey with you.

You might want to invite someone else to sit beside you in your boat and that's okay. But ultimately, they won't stay, they have their own boats.

Look after your boat.....and your boat will look after you as you now continue on this journey.

The Ball in the Box

I came across the Ball in the Box analogy about grief online. You may already know about this. If not, here's a brief description of how I see it.

In simple terms, imagine a box with a ball and a button inside. The box is you. The metal ball is your grief over a loved one. Inside the box is a magnetic button on one side. The button is pain.

The ball starts off big inside the box and is permanently pushed up against the pain button. The magnet is strong between the ball and the button.

Over time, the ball gets smaller but it is still drawn towards the pain button, often when you least expect it to be.

The period in between each hit may reduce over time, but then something will trigger it, like a song, a memory, a date, a word, an image, a smell or just a random thought….and bang, it hits against it hard, shaking the box all over the place.

Something might happen that makes the ball feel larger again and it hits the button more often. And then, one day, it shrinks down to something more manageable.

Over time, the box may fill up with another ball, and another ball. They all make space for one another. Each one finding a way to fit. Sometimes just one may hit the button, sometimes they all may hit the button. The box feels like it may explode. But it doesn't. It's strong enough. It really is.

CHAPTER 12

What Helps Me Might Help You Too

Hugs

Never underestimate the power of a hug. With the death of a loved one during lockdown, hugs were not easily available.

Not only has this pandemic taken away a loved one, it has taken away the ability to fulfil the desire and need for a hug.

I hug a lot. I'm very fortunate that I have a husband to hug, two wonderful young children who love hugs just as much as I do and some amazing friends who love hugs too. I'm lucky. There are many of you reading this who do not have this and if I could reach out and hug you right now, I would.

Hugging creates oxytocin and serotonin, the feel good hormones. We need to increase these during times of stress and grief.

Find a grief partner

I found that talking to my husband wasn't quite right. He was focused on the practical stuff, such as providing meals, making sure I got outdoors for walks, taking care of the active things such as collecting my brother's belongings from the police station and being with my parents as well as working to support us financially. He was going through his own grief and pain for very different reasons. Talking to my friends helped, but they didn't know my brother. Talking to my brother's friends and partner helped but they were immersed in their own intense grief and there were conflicts as well to deal with which caused further distress as a result.

I then reconnected with my brother's best friend from childhood. I hadn't been in touch with him for 34 years and he and Stu last saw each other in 1986! And yet, getting back in touch was meant to be. I reconnected with someone who knew my brother, knew me, knew our childhood home really well, knew our parents and, whilst he was grieving the loss of his old best friend, he understood my grief. I have been very lucky to have this person come back into my life and I strongly believe my brother arranged for this to happen because he knew he was the one person who could bring some of our happy childhood memories back to life.

However, we didn't get back in touch until two months after my brother's death and so, as I explained earlier, the way to get my thoughts and feelings out before then was to dictate on a voice recording app on my phone. Three months down the line, I listened back to the very first recording I did which was three days after his body was found, the transcript in Chapter 5. It was a real insight to hear this and reading back through the book now helps me to realise just how far I've come.

Self-Havening

The Havening Techniques® is a Psychosensory modality that works by using sensory touch to make positive changes to our own brain chemistry through a set of applied protocols.

Mostly used for trauma, PTSD/PTSI and the symptoms of these in a therapeutic setting with a qualified practitioner, it is also ideal for applying the sensory touch to self, to create calmness, relaxation and to reduce anxiety. Therapies such as EMDR, TFT and EFT have been around for many years and

Havening evolved from these methods by possibly improving upon them with the support of neuroscience.

If you want to give this a go to just put yourself in a calmer place right now, notice how you feel and cross your arms so your right hand is on your left shoulder and your left hand is on your right shoulder. A bit like giving yourself a hug.

Then stroke both arms downwards at the same time in a firm (but not too firm) rhythmic movement to the elbows. As you reach your elbow, lift your hands up back to the shoulders and place them back down as you stroke downwards again. Whilst doing this, hum a tune out loud (or in your head) or say the alphabet backwards.

Repeat the arm stroking at least 30 times. Notice what's changed. You may feel calmer, more relaxed or just neutral.

By doing this often you are lowering the body's production of the stress hormone, cortisol and creating more serotonin, the feel good hormone to help you relax and feel safe. The power of touch is incredibly healing.

As an alternative, you can rub the palms of your hands together in a rhythmic movement, or, stroke the cheeks on your face (like putting on moisturiser) and feel how comforting this feels. As humans, we instinctively know how to soothe ourselves.

There's much more involved when using Havening for therapy or healing with a practitioner, but I'm just sharing the most simplistic basics to help you feel some comfort and help change your brain chemistry in a positive calming way.

Anxiety

I love learning about the brain and how it works. Anxiety is often connected with grief and it's likely that you've experienced or are experiencing this too.

I find that when I learn about something and understand it better, it changes how I think and feel about it and this can be really helpful with anxiety and, in fact, anything to do with how our brain/ mind works.

These are just a few tips that you may find useful or helpful that have helped me:

Change your state

If you're sitting, get up. Move. Jump. Dance. Walk. Change your surroundings, your environment. The lighting. The temperature. They all have an impact on us.

Get the adrenaline moving and out of you. If you stay stuck in the same place, you'll continue feeling the same feelings. Move, scream, shout, cry, laugh. Get those emotions moving. Only when you are moving can you change direction. Movement is a regulation tool – we need to listen to what our body needs.

Unwanted thoughts

If you're in your head with unwanted thoughts, feeling overwhelmed or anxious, do this instead – count backwards from 100, sing or hum a tune. You cannot do 'thinking' whilst you're humming a tune. Give it a go. Once you've done this, then continue singing or humming and apply the Self-Havening touch above. If you can listen to a song through headphones, even better.

By releasing the feelings, you'll begin to notice your brain chemicals changing from having too much cortisol to creating serotonin and oxytocin, the feel good hormones. Continue doing this until you notice you're feeling lighter and able to breathe again and motivated to go do something, something useful, purposeful, positive, making a difference. It could be housework. Exercise. Decorating. Tidying up. Something active.

Feel the love of your loved one(s) reaching out to you in your mind and holding you tight. Know you are loved. Know you are safe, protected and cared for.

Therapy Methods

These all work in their own way, depending on the therapist, their training, experience etc. Every person grieves differently and will therefore respond differently.

There's an abundance of different therapeutic models and methods available – these are just my own personal preferences. Always be sure to check a practitioner's qualifications and testimonials first.

Grief Counsellor – ideally they should be specifically trained in suicide grief

Clinical Hypnotherapy – helps with overall wellbeing, relaxing and comforting

The Havening Techniques® – helps to clear trauma, PTSD, anxiety, negative emotions, self-comforting

Sound Healing – helps to balance and provide overall wellbeing

BreathWork – helps to release emotions, restore health and provide connection

Natural Therapy

I've applied most of those listed below in my life alongside some of the above as I feel this approach is the most beneficial for me.

Remember, it's important to reach out to others for professional help if you feel you need to.

Walking

Running

Singing

Dancing

Writing (journaling/poems/blogs/books)

Drawing/doodling/colouring/painting/crafting

Hugging (even if it's a teddy bear, or yourself, or a tree)

Meditation

Gardening

Talking

GPs are now starting to 'prescribe' taking daily walks or doing art therapy instead of handing out medications or just talking therapy.

I believe this is a positive move and, providing the support is there, this could have a positive impact for so many people.

Fresh air, being with nature, taking time to breathe, being by the sea, listening to the birds singing, gardening, even just playing in the earth............all of these are extremely effective for our wellbeing.

Trust in yourself

'You're so strong'. 'You're so brave'.

I've had several people say both of these to me and I wasn't quite sure what to make of those phrases. Am I strong? Am I brave? I don't think so.

I'm just grieving and taking each day as it comes at the moment. I don't think we truly know how we deal with something like this until we are suddenly dropped into it from a height when we least expect it and then something inside of us sparks up and pushes us along.

People will often not know what to say, especially because suicide is involved.

I try to never take anything personally so that if something is said that could be taken as upsetting or unkind, I choose not to see it as that. I just understand that people are trying to be kind and helpful and sometimes their choice of words may not come across in that way, but their intention and their hearts just want to show they care. Of course, there may be a few who are malicious in their intent and you'll know the difference between this type of person immediately, in which case, remove yourself from their company both online and offline for your own sake.

CHAPTER 13

Stop For A Moment...And Breathe

In the early days, someone said to me 'remember to breathe' and that's stayed with me ever since.

So, as you sit here, reading these words, I want you to just stop, pause.....and breathe.

Nothing else. Just breathe.

Take a really deep breath in through your nose (feel your abdomen expand and in your mind count to seven or more), hold for about four seconds then slowly let it out through your mouth (double the length of the in-breath).

Do this again and, this time, drop your shoulders, relax your jaw and just let go. Feel how it feels to just let go.

"Be Gentle On Yourself"

You may feel lighter, relief, calm, or you may cry. It's OK. Just go with it. Allow your mind and body to just 'be' for a moment.

If we shallow breath in our chests, we can end up hyperventilating or bringing on panic and anxiety. So, start noticing where you breathe and learn how to inhale as your tummy expands. Then exhale fully as your tummy deflates. It takes practice.

Breathe life........breathe love.

CHAPTER 14

A Letter to My Brother...

I'm learning to live with your loss.

There's no right or wrong way, it's different every day.

I'm feeling all the emotions, expressing them through:

Tears

Art

Music

Writing

Talking

Breathing

Walking,

And trusting my heart

Your physical presence that's no longer here, pains me when you can't be near

But, when I focus on your spirit through love,

Your signs, messages and hugs from above,

I sense and I know where you are and although I can't see you or hug you

I know you are here and never ever far

I'm learning….

Every day in some small or big way

I'm learning…

Learning to live with what happened

Learning to accept your decision

Learning to live with my grief

And learning to live with new beliefs

I love you my darling brother

I miss you, until we meet again

Your sister xxxx

Chapter 15

Signs & Messages

I've always had a fascination with the powers of the Universe.

My brother and I used to have conversations where we would ask each other 'why am I me and why are you you and why are we brother and sister and why am I not you instead?' And we would go down the rabbit hole discussing the endless possibilities.

I've touched on a few of these 'coincidences' in a previous chapter which from now on I will call 'signs' because that's what I believe them to be so I want to list and explain each one in chronological order.

1) **In 2016 I'm pregnant with twins. Boy and girl twins. Twins do not run in either family.**

Is this the Universe preparing our family for my brother departing four years later? Providing me with a son and daughter together who have that close bond as brother and sister and giving our parents their only grandchildren, one of each.

When I see them interacting and playing together, it transports me back to my childhood and is both heartwarming and emotional.

2) **January 2020, my brother and I become attorneys for our parents' LPA; the solicitor comments 'Let's hope nothing happens to either of your children before you die…..'**

That's quite a statement to be made and to hear.

3) **29 April 2020 (my brother's birthday) – I receive a text message from a number I don't recognise saying my brother has added me as an emergency contact. I've still no idea what this was for.**

Why did he do this?

4) **30 May 2020 my three year old daughter draws a picture of Nana, Grandad, Aunty Louise and Uncle Stu. The picture of Stu clearly shows a line going up from around his neck….**

Did she see the future in her mind and draw this?

5) **14 June 2020 – The Meltdown at Bedgebury Pinetum. At 11am (the time Stu left his home that day), his three year old niece clung to a memorial tree during our trip to Bedgebury and refused to let go. She's never had a meltdown before so this was totally out of character. At the same time, her twin brother was desperate to go back to the car to go home and was also distressed but he wouldn't leave his sister.**

Did the twins sense something was wrong? I felt something in my heart when I saw the man's abandoned sunglasses on the ground by the tree. Was that a sign connecting my brother to his tree perhaps?

6) **On the same day, the heartbreaking news of the body of the local taxi driver who had been missing for over a week had been found sadly deceased. I remember commenting to my husband and putting my hand on his shoulder to say how incredibly sad this was. I was possibly more sensitive to this because of**

my brother being a taxi driver too and the night before I'd heard the helicopter flying overhead in the local search.

Did my brother hear the news too on his way to the forest? I don't normally listen or watch the news and I can't remember how I heard about this but I believe I was meant to hear it because of what was about to happen to us as a family. A month before, I'd also heard the tragic news of a local boy who had been found in a local park.

He too had died by suicide. There's the saying that 'things happen in threes'....

7) **Before the twins went to bed, they took some flowers off a nearby plant and scattered them in the herb planter (there were 12 flower heads and I wonder if the number 12 is significant at all? A connection to my brother, possibly the time he died? I don't know – it's just a thought.)**

Were they scattering flowers for a different reason that they didn't know about?

8) After the twins were in bed, I watched a repeat episode of Downton Abbey....the one where one of the siblings dies. I remember messaging my friends to say I'd forgotten about that particular episode and it made me tearful.

Little did I know, my brother had probably already died whilst I was watching this.

9) 15 June 2020 – I didn't take any photographs. I've got over 30k photos on my iPhone and I take pictures every day. Why didn't I take any photos? I can't even remember anything about that day.

It's almost as if the day after he died didn't exist but, at that point, I didn't know he had died or was in fact was missing.

10) 17 June 2020 – We visited Ashdown Forest to search for him but the torrential rain stopped us from going into the forest

If it hadn't been raining, could we have potentially found him?

11) **21 June 2020** – Telling the twins about their uncle. I remember sitting on the sofa where Stu had last sat with the twins. I explained why I had been so upset during the week and that 'uncle Stu has very sadly died'. Twin two sat very still and, looking directly ahead with a different tone of voice, said 'He put something around his neck'. Naturally, I was somewhat taken aback by this statement because there was absolutely no way he would know this. I'd had conversations with my husband and on the phone but they were always out of the room and I had never once mentioned the cause of death. I asked him how he knew this and he replied 'because I saw him'. He then continued to say 'he was sad' when I asked how he seemed. All the time he was talking, his sister was drawing a picture on the magi draw board. I can't remember what it was as I was totally focused on his words.

Were the first 10 of these early signs that lead up to my brother's passing? And is my brother now communicating through the twins and by other means?

The white feathers that appear at significant times or places. The songs that suddenly come on the radio that have key words or meanings. The faces in the clouds. The pictures falling off the bookcase. The smoke detector in the house going off for no reason. I've had so many messages and connections with my brother since. I'll share these in my next book as there are so many.

Something I recall thinking a lot in the first few weeks and months was 'Has Stu sent me something through Amazon as a way to explain or say sorry?'

Every time there was a knock at the door after he died, I wondered whether it was a letter or a parcel from Stuart that he'd arranged the day he died. I kept longing and hoping. But nothing ever came. There's been nothing, no note, no goodbye, nothing.

I often keep thinking something from my brother will just turn up out of the blue. I'm not sure what, but it gives me a level of comfort that I can't really explain.

CHAPTER 16

Reflecting

Today, I was sent a couple of photographs that had just been taken at my brother's home with the Christmas tree up in the living room.

Yes it's November. But this is the year 2020.

That was the home where my brother lived for 18 months, where he sat and watched TV, or napped on the sofa with the dog, or played silly games. He laughed. He ate sweets. He looked out the window. He chatted...................he lived there. He was alive there. Alive.

Now, he's gone. Gone. There's a Christmas tree at his house now but he didn't help to put it up this year. He didn't put the decorations on it. He isn't there in the room to sit with it and admire it and get that Christmas feeling.

It's a room. It still has life in it. Life going on still. Voices. Sounds. Music. Movement. Activity. Laughter. Tears. Sadness. It's all there. But he's not.

His physical presence isn't there. He won't walk through the door or sit on the sofa anymore or make someone else laugh or just feel better if they were feeling low.

And yet.............he does see and has seen everything in that room, from his new position as spirit. He has sat on that sofa. He has been making people laugh with the memories. He has added a few decorations to the tree because he held your hand whilst you did it. He is moving around the room with you because he walks with you and puts his arm around you when you're feeling down.

He desperately wants to reach out and hug you but he can't because you can't hug back. So he just hopes you sense him around and feel him close without actually seeing him in person. Because he is there. He is there. He wants you to keep going and enjoy the Christmas season with hope, with love, with laughter and plenty of sweets! He wants you to smile and laugh and talk to him and talk about him and remember him. He's with you.

He'll be the reason a bauble drops to the floor. The reason a light flickers. The reason a candle dims and then flickers back to life again. The knocking twitching sound behind the walls. The shadow passing in the background. The tap dripping. The cold breeze that suddenly flits passed and makes you shudder. The warmth you feel as you snuggle down with a blanket. The reason the doorbell rings and no one is there. The tap on the window. See that bird? That was him. The insect walking across the floor………yep that was him. Look out the window at night………….see the brightest star?

That's him, shining bright, willing you to smile and feel comfort. Go out into the garden during the day and look at the clouds. See how they change? See the slideshow of images? He's doing that for you.

He's wanting to make you smile and laugh and love. Open a book and find a page, a word. That's a message. Listen to the radio.

That song that just came on, that's for you. You'll hear his name spoken out loud when you're out shopping and you'll stop and turn. You'll look. You'll wonder, you'll hope. He wanted you to know he's there with you too. When you sleep at night, as you close your eyes, you'll see his eyes. He'll watch you sleep so you know you are safe all night through.

Go to a tree and talk to that tree. Observe it. Touch it. Hug it if you want to. Let the tree help you to breathe. Allow the tree to give you strength, comfort, energy, support, love, life. Make that tree, your tree, your loved one's tree. Sit by your tree as often as you need to. Let it bring you comfort. Feel the life, the energy. The tree is offering everything you need to keep going. Take it. Take it as you breathe. Embrace this connection. Hold onto it and, as you leave, know that this connection is in your heart, your soul, from this point forwards. Know that you have the power to connect to others, just like that tree. You too can reach out and offer love, hope, support, kindness, energy, comfort to others who need this just like you. Because the connection is real. They did this, just like the tree. Always reaching out to help others. Always offering help and support, love and comfort, encouragement and motivation. Your tree, whenever you visit it, will give you this in abundance for yourself and will give you the permission that it's OK to share this with others. It's OK. It's all OK.

Believe in yourself. Breathe. You are connected. They are with you. And you will be able to walk stronger each day, just taking one day at a time. It's not a race. There's no winner or loser because there's no end. It's a walk you're doing together and one day, one day, you may find you can walk by yourself. One day. But not now. Now is time to accept the support, their support. Let it help you. Let them help you. Let this help others.

Another Letter to Stuart

It's the 2nd day of December

I'm busy keeping busy

Decorations, writing cards, organising presents

Planning things, organising things, finding things I'd forgotten

One minute you were here, the next you were gone.

June seems only like yesterday; Christmas seems so far away

But it's not. It's December now and I don't know where you are.

You're not here. I want to send you your Christmas card and Christmas present.

The twins want to see their favourite uncle and laugh and play.

Mum and Dad want you to just pop by as you always did, just to say hi or get them some shopping or do some DIY.

But you're not here. You're not here and my tears keep on coming.

I don't like it just being me without my sibling, without my brother.

I have to focus on you as spirit. I can't see you, but I sense you're around.

I can't touch you but I know you move things and often drop things on the ground.

I speak to you but you don't speak back although I hear your voice in my head and I know you're listening.

So keep leaving the feathers, keep making things disappear or past things reappear. Play those songs that remind me of you, show me those signs and messages as often as you want as they help me, they help me in this time of need.

I still don't understand why, no one does..............
do you?

But it's too late now, you've gone and our hearts are broken and I know you didn't want to break them. There are no answers now, only memories and hope.

We live on and we will make you proud, as we are of you. We love you Stu. We miss you. We think of you.

So, when I cry, do something to make me smile to keep me going for a while. Do the same for Mum and Dad and all those who love you, who miss you, who think of you.

Here's to you Stu,

I love you and miss you,

Your little sister x

CHAPTER 17

Why I Don't Want 2020 To End

Someone said to me 'I bet you'll be relieved when 2020 is over.'

And that hit me. Not in the way I expected it to.

It hit me because my immediate response was 'NO'. No, I don't want 2020 to finish...........ever.

Because, in 2020, my brother was still alive for the first six months. He was still alive and I could speak to him, see him, hear him, message him..............and he'd respond. He would answer. He would smile, he would laugh. He would be there.

2020 is a year I will never forget. It has changed the world. It has changed our own worlds. It has changed everything.

Just writing this now, fills me with so much emotion. A mix of happy memories, joy, life, love, blended in with tears of sadness, feelings of sorrow, loss, emptiness.

I'm holding on to 2020 because it feels like I'm holding onto my brother. When the clock strikes midnight on 31 December 2020, I will cry. I will cry my heart out. I will feel like I've lost my brother all over again. I will feel he is further away. I can see my hand holding his and he's letting go. He's letting go and drifting away and I'm alone. My heart is broken. I'm alone.

When I think about what our parents are going through, I cannot even begin to imagine. How are they still going, doing everyday life? How? How do they do that? It breaks my heart to know they are hurting and in so much pain and I can't make it better for them. No one can.

This is when I have to breathe. And remind myself that Stuart has transitioned, he didn't die, he just transitioned back into his spirit. He's well, he's watching over us, he's with me now. I just can't physically see him, and that's what hurts right now. I want to see him so much. I want to give him such a big hug and tell him I love him. I want to tell him he was and still is the best best best brother and I'm sorry

I never told him, but I hope he knows this, I really hope he knows this. I have tears flowing down my face right now. I need to breathe. Just breathe.

Stuart has given me the courage to be me. To live my dreams. We are brought up to think that dreams are not real and we need to focus on academic achievements and such like. Sod that.

Our life is our life. It's what we make it. It's not for someone else to tell us what to do, how we should be, how we should think. We are all perfectly capable of being our true authentic selves and I think that's what Stuart was trying to do and be. Love and kindness – two of Stu's biggest strengths. He made sure others felt loved and were cared for. He was and is an angel of kindness and I will carry this on for you my brother, I will continue this for you with every single person I meet. That's a promise.

So, I'm still working through 2020 and thinking how I will be able to transition to 2021 in a more serving, beneficial and positive way.

I'm not there yet…………..one day at a time, one moment at a time, one step at a time. One thought can make all the difference.

Today, I say thank you to 2020 for opening up my eyes to believe in myself and to help others to believe in themselves too.

2020 has actually been the biggest, most impactful, insightful and challenging year so far.   Life is precious.   Life is short.   Live your life now, not tomorrow, not next year or in 10 years............live your life now, because you are you and that's what makes each and every one of us special.

CHAPTER 18

Six Months of Grieving, Six Months Since He's Been Gone

Six months on and I'm noticeably distracting myself from thinking of my brother because, as soon as I think of him, I get very emotional. So I've started noticing as soon as the thought appears I then push it away or distract myself by humming a tune, or changing the subject when talking to someone.

I know this is just all part of the grief but it makes me feel a bit guilty for not thinking about him as much as I had been doing on a daily basis.

The realisation of what's happened is really sinking in now. I thought I'd accepted this a few weeks ago but I think that was just the start of the process of accepting he has died.

My brother has died.

My brother is gone.

It's hard writing those sentences. He's gone. It feels so final. And yet, still it seems unreal even though in other moments it seems very real.

I seem to have tuned out of my spiritual guidance for a short time whilst I process the facts and emotions and events that happened here in life. I feel as though I want to go back over it all, not sure why. Perhaps to try to make some sense of it but, of course, that won't happen will it? I'm clutching at straws. I'm trying to find answers, but I never will, will I? So why am I looking, searching, hoping? Perhaps it was because he was missing at first, so I went through that process of looking, searching and hoping? I don't know.

Today actually marks two 'anniversaries'; one year since I last saw my brother in person and six months since his body was found.

Life got in the way after Christmas 2019.

We saw each other on Wednesday 18 December 2019.

January, February was the usual business with a new year, work, kids, life etc.

March came and we planned to go to visit but then lockdown hit the UK so that never happened.

COVID-19 stopped us from seeing each other in person ever again. Mum and Dad last saw their son at the beginning of March. When they waved goodbye, he was standing on his doorstep waving back. That was the last time they ever saw him…

We did our last ever FaceTime together at the end of March and, after that, April, May and June, it was just weekly text messages.

I never saw you ever again Stu.

The only time I hear his voice now is through captured video footage.

I keep hoping to stumble across recordings or photos that I haven't heard or seen before, but that's a very rare find now. But I still keep hoping….

I still can't quite get my head around any of this.

I don't understand.

If he'd died from natural causes, I'd still be upset but I wouldn't keep asking these questions….

What was so bad that you had to take away your life?

Would anything have changed your mind?

Do you regret doing it?

Do you wish someone could have saved you?

You see, there's the grief from his death; he's no longer physically here. I've lost my brother. Then there's the grief, the pain, from how he died. It doesn't make any sense. It probably never will.

But I'm human. He's my blood relative. A part of me died that day too. So I want to know, to understand, to make sense of it all.

We expected our parents to die before us. That we would be there for each other when each parent passed away. That we would continue our family line. But my brother didn't have any children. So I'm the closest blood relative when our parents die, so I have to carry on that part of him through me and through my children, his niece and nephew. Otherwise, it just stops. The end of the line. How can someone who made such a positive impact on so many lives, just be gone and then there's nothing? How can this be?

My brain keeps trying to process it all. Memories keep popping up. Other memories then disappear and fade away. How do I keep all our 46 years of memories alive and continuing to our future generations? Or do I just have to accept that they will die with me when I go to?

I'm finding it harder to look at photographs at the moment. Seven months since he's been gone and some days I start to think the reality of his death has started to sink in, but then on other days I still just can't believe it all. Some days I go to send him a text and then suddenly it hits me.........he won't answer.

It feels so lonely because no one else knows how this feels. Everyone grieves their own loss, even if they're grieving for the same person. We all have different memories, feelings, emotions, reminders. All different, but all equally painful to each of us individually.

There's an emptiness....a void.

Nothing. Nothingness. There's no word to describe how I feel right now. Just tears. I'll let the tears flow.

I look up at the many photos of him I have on my desk and see him smiling. He's smiling at me. And yet, I'm here crying back at him. Why? Why is he still smiling and I'm crying? Does he want me to smile too? I will. I do. Just not today, or at least not at the moment. I just need to let the tears flow. I have conversations with him in my head and I hear his voice. I know he's sorry. I know he wishes he could make it all better for us. He wants to shout out to say he's OK and that he's with us and we'll be OK too. I feel his hand reach out to hold mine, just like we did when we were little. He was always supposed to be here, to share special times, sad times, to see his niece and nephew grow up. Hold their little hands too. Protect them just like he protected me and our Mum and Dad.

I have no more words..........

CHAPTER 19

So What Does Suicide Leave Behind?

Why did I call this book 'What Suicide Left Behind?'
This is why...........

I could focus on all the intense sadness, grief, loss,
heartache, pain, questions, disbelief, loneliness,
emptiness.....the list goes on as you well know.

I could quite easily do this. But what will that do for
me? What will that do for you, for others?

Will it just keep me in those sad dark feelings and
emotions? Just going round and round in circles
feeling unable to break that cycle, escape the pain,
unable to breathe or just look up.

Is this how I want to live? Is this how my parents want
to see their now only living child? Will this help my
children? Does my husband want to live with
someone who is suffering daily?

Of course not.

But, we have to be allowed the space to grieve in our own way. Not be told how and when and where. Others can't truly understand or empathise unless they have been there with us and, even then, there's only so much they can understand.

My brother, and what has happened, has taught me so much about him, myself, others, and life and death.

I find myself with so much more empathy for others. I have more time for others and I listen, really listen. And I check in with friends and family too…..are they really OK or just saying what they think we want to hear? I always follow this up with 'are you really OK?' and the reply may differ to their initial response. You've just given space to that person so that it's OK to open up and express how they really feel. This is what we all need more of. We need others to make it OK for us to be raw, be authentic, be real. There's no shame in expressing our emotions.

A moment will try to present itself. A moment of lightness. You may not even notice it at first. You may not expect it, or want it. You may want to stay where you are because, whilst it's not comfortable, it's become familiar. Because you want to hold onto your loved one, and you don't know how else to do this.

You don't know how to be, how to get through each day, how to breathe, how to move, how to change one step at a time, one day at a time.

But sit quiet for a moment and just focus on your breathing. Nothing else. Just breathing. And ask 'how can I.......?' And allow yourself to find and ask your own question. And then just let it go.

Leave your question with the Universe. Let your guardian angel deliver your question to your loved one and they will answer. They will answer at the right moment. The moment you need to hear it, you want to hear it. And then, and only then, will you listen.

And when you listen, you will feel something different, something inside you has changed.

Just a little something.

But it's enough to give you something else to hold onto now.

Reach out and hold onto this feeling, this moment.

Because this is your first step, your first moment, helping you out of that dark lonely space, holding your hand and guiding you forwards but only at the pace that's right for you.

My brother passing by suicide leaves behind:

Grief

Pain

Healing

Love

Courage to learn

Self-discovery

The ability to see life differently/a different outlook

What's really important/what really matters

Empathy

Compassion

Time for others

Connection

Suicide has left behind a purpose, a passion, a mission.

Grief and suicide are still uncomfortable subjects for people. I'm on a mission to change this and make suicide grief more openly acceptable and less judged or compared or stigmatised.

Suicide is on the increase and there's no stereotypical person that many people think it only affects. It truly can happen to anyone.

That phrase 'I never thought this would happen to me', how many times have we heard others say that? I've heard it hundreds of times about all sorts of different things. And yet, I've only just realised that I can say this now too.

We can learn to let go of the pain and suffering whilst not letting go of the love and the memories. I know how it feels to think that if we let go of the pain, we are letting go of them. We are not. We never 'move on', we 'move forward' at our own gentle steady pace. The bond with our loved one never dies and we can find a way to continue that connection in our everyday lives. Give yourself permission to open your mind to possibilities of how that connection will show up for you. The memories and the love we have, live on in you, not in the pain.

CHAPTER 20

Words Of Comfort

Scattered throughout social media are many posts with words of comfort and support.

Here are some of my favourites that appear on many different places without the original source so I'm unable to credit them, along with some of my own…..

You cannot accidentally 'remind' me of my loved who has died because I will never forget. But you can 'remind' me that you are remembering them too and that's what helps get me through. Mention their name, talk about them, remember them. That's the best gift.

You can speak a thousand words and some people will not hear you and understand.

There are others though who will just know, just understand,

and you don't even have to say anything.

Train yourself to find the blessing in everything

Train yourself to find **gratitude** in everything

…We become controlling when we feel out of control

If you can't do anything about it, why hold onto it?

Let it go.

Otherwise you'll become a prisoner in your own mind.

Thoughts become things – pay attention to what you focus on

Where focus goes….energy flows

If I depart whilst you're still here

Let me go, have no fear

For I have gone from sight but not from your heart

I live on in a different energy but we are never apart

Just whisper my name anytime you need me

I'll be with you, I promise, ……

What is a brother or sister?

*He/she is the one you've grown up with but never
outgrew*

The one you trust

That familiar face that's always there

*The keeper of your childhood memories to cherish
and share*

*The one you always just assumed would be there,
past, present and future*

When your sibling dies, you lose a part your past,
your present and your future

Never let anything or anyone put out the light that shines within you

from the moment you were born

Vulnerability connects us; *perfection separates us*

When you've been lost in the dark,

know that there is someone out there willing

and wanting to help you switch that light back on in your eyes.

Let them help you.

Have you ever wondered that the advice you give to others may be advice you need to hear for yourself? People around us are sometimes a projection of our own lives.

The universe is giving you signs and messages every day.

Some days you'll notice them, some days you won't.

Once you tune in to these, you'll learn to listen, see and feel them more often.   Notice the patterns.

Trust in the universe and trust in yourself,

…because you are the universe.

Sometimes we just need someone to be there. Not to say anything.

Just to be there.

Just so we can feel loved, supported and cared for.

You will live as long as I live

You will be remembered with every beat of my heart

As long as I live, you will be loved

*....and one day everything changed. It took just **one day**.*

With every suffering comes a message;

discover what that message is,

it may just help you....

Do you refer to your loved one in the past tense or present tense?

"My brother loved this" or "my brother love**s** this".

Notice the difference when you say this....

Repeat after me:

I am not my childhood

I am not my past

I am not my traumas

I am not other people's judgements and opinions

I am not my family or friends

I am not the victim

I am not the villain

My past does not define me

I have the power within me to learn and grow and heal

I define who I am

I define who I will become

I write my own story, not history

I choose to live in a beautiful state, no matter what

Where do I find you?

You'll find me in between each breath,

each step, each word, each thought.

People around you will behave differently now you are grieving.

Notice the ones who struggle with your grief.

Perhaps they have never experienced such painful complex grief.

Notice the ones who regularly check in on you.

They have probably been there and are still going through their own grief journey(s).

Notice the ones who appear to have left your life.

They are probably unable to deal with your grief for their own personal reasons and that's okay.

Don't take it personally.

It's their world, let them live it and only invite them back into yours if you wish, in the future.

There's the therapists, colleagues, family members – all doing their thing.

Then there's you, you've changed and yet deep down, you are still you. Those who really care, will know that.

It's hard to turn the page knowing you won't be in the next chapter.

But actually, you can make an appearance,

just in a different form.

I'll never live each new chapter without you showing up somehow.

I'll write you in and

I'll never leave you out.

There is something unique and beautiful about a person who grows from their pain and grief and uses the lessons from their experiences to help themselves and others. It doesn't matter how or why you fell. Be the example to others that they too can overcome that mountain.

If you focus on hurt, you will continue to suffer

If you focus on the lesson, you will begin to grow

Sometimes it's the happy memories that can hurt the most

Some people awaken to spirituality because they can't stand the suffering anymore

One day you will thank yourself for never giving up

No one sees what you see or thinks what you think

Even if they see it or think it too

Memories of you often sneak out of my eyes and roll down my cheeks.

Always help or be kind to someone else, you might be the only one who does

How to live in a bad state:

Talk to yourself negatively

Be the victim

Blame everything and everyone for all the bad stuff

Repeat daily for the rest of your life

Or you could choose to learn how to:

Talk to yourself positively

Be authentic

Know that you cannot always control everything going on around you but you can control how you react and respond

Repeat daily for the rest of your life

I may have died but I've not gone away

For I live on with you.......always

Through your eyes I see what you see

Through your ears I hear what you hear

When you speak, my voice speaks through you

With words of love, kindness and truth

In your heart, I feel what you feel

Look after yourself, find ways to heal

When you see a friend of mine,

know that they still love me and miss me,

like you

Give them a hug, hold their hands,

say my name

and you'll both feel my warmth all the way through

CHAPTER 21

A Journal for Treasured Memories – Your Space to Remember and Reflect

The following pages are you for you record special memories. Memories you want to remember, always. Write them down to strengthen them and make them feel closer.

Write their name, their nickname(s), anything you called them

Rogan 's favourite hobbies

Climbing

fixing stuff - bikes, computers etc...

Watching tv / films

Rog _____'s favourite music Indie /rap

Trainspotting album
Rocketman
lil peep , Juiceworld, XXX...
Catfish and the bottlemen

Rog _____'s favourite movies

Trainspotting
fight club
didn't mind marvel
Suicide squad 2

Rogan 's favourite food/drink

litterally anything - beside specific
oven chips

dessert food / bakery treats

Rogs 's favourite clothing/colours

black / white / gray
or would wear light colours
like baby blue, baby pink, lilac

_Rog_____'s favourite sayings/jokes/phrases/words

"Chavey", "naw dinny", "kezza"
"da baby? lets gooo" "doi doi doi"
"This dug min" "Scran"

_Rog_____'s favourite places to visit

Holland

Rogan 's favourite people

Dad, mum, cammy, Reece, Sonny, fil, Keiron
Aidan, Kye, gran, grandad, logan

_____'s favourite (other)

Moments I will always treasure:

- 7th August, Train, cinema, drinks, mcd's with aidan and leah
- 🖊 Smoking in your car with you watching Rick and morty
- Watching xmen and slasher films all week when mum & dad were gone
- Holland in total
- Whenever we cried together
- nightshifts / walking home together

My first memory of you / us:

When you were born, going in
gift shop for a 'its a boy' balloon

Walking down hallway

Mum ~~was~~ holding you on chair
In hallway (?)

My last memory of you / us:

My letter to you now (for you to read in heaven/ spirit/paradise/…….) not yet

I'll come back

How I will always remember you/honour you:

If you want your loved one to send you signs and messages, write down here what you think they will be / what you would like them to be. Then notice what happens over the coming weeks, months, years ahead…..

- music so far
- butterfly, specifically orange
- lights flicker
- remi staring into random spots in room

Little Daily Reminders of Things I Can Do To Help Me Heal / To Uplift Me When Needed / My Daily Wellness Mantra:

I'll see him in an alternative universe when I die

Space to write anything you wish – go with the flow:

Final Words

I hope my book has helped you in some way. As you now know, I wrote this through the first six months of grieving the loss of my only sibling through suicide and so it's written entirely from a broken heart whilst in shock.

Alongside writing this, I'm in the process of setting up a 'Suicide Loss Survivor Community' which is an online and offline space for us to all to come together and express our emotions through singing, dancing, art, writing, running, healing, meditation and more, in a safe and supported community. Anyone with suicidal thoughts is especially welcome, in the hope we can save lives and give hope for a better future.

The launch of this book and the community, which is called Paradisium, meaning 'into paradise' (The Paradisium Tree of Hope & Healing), was due to be 29 April 2021. This is the date my brother would have been 49 here on Earth and now instead celebrates a heavenly (or paradise) birthday. However, the launch date is now on the first anniversary of his passing, 14 June 2021.

The name Paradisium came about with the help of my brother's childhood friend, Claire Harris, who I am so grateful to.

Claire and I have also created specialised Grief Support Cards that offer hope and support and spiritual connections to those who have lost loved ones to suicide.

I'm now writing a second book as I felt there was too much content to include in this first one and I'm now also further on into my grief/healing journey.

My next book focuses on the afterlife, connections, mediums, healing methods/techniques, first anniversaries (birthdays, Christmas, the date he died and was found) and dreams (like the one where I dreamt he died, woke up and thought thank goodness it was just a dream and then realised it was real).

I am truly grateful to you for reading my grief journey (part 1). I genuinely hope this helps you and has offered some comfort and support as well as knowing that you are not alone on this journey.

We all understand and we are all connected. Let's come together and use our voices. Talk, share, reach out. You are not alone.

Together we remember; together we are stronger.

Let all that you do, be done with love.

Linzi x (& Stu RIP x)

Those who grieve well, live well.

Never in a million years

did I think I would write a book…

Never in a million years

did I think my brother would die by suicide…

Professional Acknowledgements:

With thanks to Steve Crabb, Dr Ronald Ruden, Paul McKenna Phd, Dr Richard Bandler, John and Kathleen La Valle, June O'Driscoll, Tina Taylor and Michael Neill for all their training and mentoring over the years which has helped me to build a resilient mindset to be able to navigate my own grief journey and share my learnings with you.

Resources:

Suicide Loss Survivors Online Support Community:

www.paradisium.co.uk

Offering weekly online choir, art classes, dance videos, meditations, hypnotic tracks (for sleep, relaxation, comfort and support), mindset coaching, healing workshops and more. This is the alternative or complimentary support to grief counselling and medication.

Facebook Group:

www.facebook.com/groups/whatsuicideleftbehind

Facebook Page:

www.facebook.com/whatsuicideleftbehind

Instagram:

www.instagram.com/linzi_meaden_suicide_grief/

Clubhouse Audio App:

@linzimeaden

"The Pivotal Moment Club"

"Evolving Through Grief Club"

Weekly conversations (interactive podcasts) discussing suicide grief, sibling loss, hope and healing, life changing moments, the afterlife, signs and messages and much more.

Suicide Prevention/Suicide Bereavement Charities:

RunningSpace (promoting life, beating suicide):

runningspace.org/

I am setting up a RunningSpace club in my local area (Tunbridge Wells, Kent) – there are various clubs throughout the UK.

SOBs (survivors of bereavement by suicide):

uksobs.org/

Therapeutic/Healing Resources:

The Havening Techniques®:

www.havening.org/

Trauma & Anxiety Therapy & Coaching:

chrismeaden.com/

My personal 'alternative' book recommendations (for adults and children):

Journey of Souls by Michael Newton PhD

What the Dead are Dying to Teach Us by Claire Broad

The Boy, the Mole, The Fox and The Horse by Charlie Mackesy

The Four Agreements by Don Miguel Ruiz

The Invisible String by Patrice Karst

The Memory Tree by Britta Teckentrup

The Midnight Library – Matt Haig (note this is fictional)

Suicide Grief Care Parcels

Sending parcels of love instead of flowers:

www.paradisium.co.uk

(supporting local / small businesses)

THE AUTHORS:

Linzi: Born in Bearsted Kent in 1974, Linzi now lives in Royal Tunbridge Wells with her husband Chris, a trauma therapist, and their young twins.

She is a qualified Coach, Hypnotherapist and Havening Techniques® practitioner.

She regularly appears on podcasts, Clubhouse talks and other social media channels sharing her grief journey to help to end the stigma of suicide and bereavement and to be a voice for those grieving the loss of loved ones, especially siblings.

She is the founder of Paradisium (The Tree of Hope & Healing) – a community for suicide loss survivors to come together for hope and healing as an alternative to talk therapy and medication. She has also created grief care parcels to gift to those bereaved by suicide.

Stuart (April 1972 – June 2020): With the same childhood home as his sister, Stuart (also known as Stu, Stuie, Stu-Pot) loved the coast and moved to Eastbourne, East Sussex. A keen fisherman (carp), car and motorbike fanatic, as well as a lover of nature and animals, Stu was always the first person to lend a hand to help others. He loved nothing more than making others smile and to see them happy. He was the best listener and motivator, always looking for the positive in any situation. His selfless kind deeds and big heart will continue through the loved ones he left behind.

Reviews

"This is a book that I wish had been written when I lost my brother to suicide over 30 years ago. Linzi has managed to harness her own feelings of loss, whilst enabling others faced with the same devastation to park their feelings here in this supportive space. She turns hopelessness into 'hope' and darkness into 'light', whilst also illuminating a pathway through some very practical sides of losing a loved one in this way. Compelling, heartfelt and sensitive to the core"

Louise Ktoris – Suicide Loss and Sibling Loss Survivor

"This beautiful book is an intimate and candid account written with raw honesty about grief after suicide. Grief is a subject no one can understand until they personally experience the often raw visceral emotions, the roller coaster of thoughts and waves of endless questions of 'why' or 'what if'. Linzi writes with a heart wrenching honesty as she shares her journey of grief after losing her beloved brother to suicide. With every word left on these pages, Linzi leaves a trail of white feathers for readers to follow on their own journey through their sorrow but also towards understanding and healing."

Steve Crabb - Author, Master Trainer of NLP and Clinical Hypnotist

"Linzi invites us into her inner world of a profound and touching personal journey of loss, faith, strength and hope, guiding the reader into the path of healing."

Chantal Brosens – Therapist and Author

Printed in Great Britain
by Amazon

71538716R00113